SAM

SAM

THE ONE AND ONLY SAM SNEAD

AL BARKOW

TAYLOR TRADE PUBLISHING
Lanham • New York • Boulder • Toronto • Plymouth, UK

Frontis photos: In this sequence of Sam's swing in his late prime, we see his clean turn or pivot in the backswing, and then his unique "sit," his downward push in the downswing that stabilized his body and created a foundation on which he could deliver his tremendously powerful blow to the ball. *Ron Muszalski*

Published by Taylor Trade Publishing
An imprint of The Rowman & Littlefield Publishing Group, Inc.
4501 Forbes Boulevard, Suite 200, Lanham, Maryland 20706
http://www.rlpgtrade.com

Estover Road, Plymouth PL6 7PY, United Kingdom

Distributed by National Book Network

British Library Cataloguing in Publication Information Available

Library of Congress Cataloging-in-Publication Data
Barkow, Al.
  Sam : the one and only Sam Snead / Al Barkow.
    p. cm.
  Includes index.
  ISBN 978-1-58979-524-2 (pbk. : alk. paper) — ISBN 978-1-58979-596-9 (electronic)
    1. Snead, Sam, 1912– 2. Golfers—United States—Biography. I. Title. II. Title: One and only Sam Snead.
  GV964.S6B37 2010
  796.352092—dc22
  [B]
                                                              2010020857

⊚ ™ The paper used in this publication meets the minimum requirements of American National Standard for Information Sciences—Permanence of Paper for Printed Library Materials, ANSI/NISO Z39.48-1992.

Printed in the United States of America

CONTENTS

FOREWORD

SAM SNEAD DESERVES A THOROUGH AND HONEST biography, and Al Barkow is the right guy to write it because he seems to have a good feel for those of us who came up in the game and in life through the Great Depression of the 1930s. Sam Snead was a product of those hard times and of a part of the country that was isolated from the social mainstream. The times and the geography had a strong influence on how Sam lived his life, on his value system, and how he was perceived by the public.

Sam was a very big celebrity not only in golf but also in all of sports. There were very few people in his time who could fill a stadium or a golf course with spectators, and Sam was one of them. He was just so good at the game, and looked so good playing, you had to go see it for yourself. Of course, that was the only way you could see him and others in the days before television, but I think the sports fans of that era had an advantage in that respect. To see Sam in the flesh, and to hear and see the sound and flight of the golf ball when he hit it, simply cannot be captured on the "tube." I can't think of another great athlete in any game who had that capacity. Joe DiMaggio, maybe, chasing a fly ball; but Joe looked like he was working when he was at bat. Sam never looked strained, and it set him apart from the rest of us. He was a winner not just because he had a pretty golf swing and could hit the ball a long way—a very long way. He was a winner, a big winner, because he knew how to *play*, how to put shots together, and could maintain a very high level of concentration. It was often said of Sam that he was a poor putter, especially from up close, and couldn't handle the pressure. Well, how does someone win all those tournaments Sam won if he can't putt and can't make putts when he needs them?

But maybe more than anything, Sam absolutely loved to play and to compete. It was that which made him so distinctive a player and personality. And yet, I'm not sure people saw that fierceness in him. Sam had this jaunty sort of look about him, with his straw hat and country-boy sayings delivered with a sly smile, but underneath all of that, he was as tough as they come. The thing about Sam and golf was that he saw the whole game. I read once about a pool shark who said he didn't see the cue ball, the other balls, the pockets, he saw the total game. That's the way Sam was about golf.

Sam was kind of a phenomenon. He had a special gift for golf and made the most of it. He loved a crowd and entertained people with his storytelling, but like every great player or anyone of a creative nature, he had a lot of loner in him. He loved having a crowd around him, loved telling his stories and getting laughs, enjoyed showing off his game to the gallery, but he could do without all that. People like Sam, like a Michelangelo or a Beethoven, don't need people around them. They like their own company and are so sure of themselves they don't feel a need to share their thoughts, their problems, and their inner life with others. This gives them an air of mystery. Now that Sam is gone, some of that mystery can be unveiled, because people do like some insight on special people. Al Barkow has done that with his biography of Sam; it's a story of Sam he would never tell himself, but one that needs to be told. It will enrich the memory of him for those who knew him and saw him play and give him a presence he deserves.

Jack Burke Jr.

PREFACE

THERE ARE CERTAIN EXPERIENCES ONE HAS IN A LIFETIME that can be classified as privileges. One of those for me was getting to watch Sam Snead in his prime hitting golf balls. Those who never had this experience have truly missed something. To be sure, they can watch it on film or video, but it is simply not the same.

I had that opportunity as a teenage caddie in the 1940s at the fabulous Tam O' Shanter Country Club, in a north suburb of Chicago. For two consecutive weeks every summer all the great golfers in the world, men and women, pros and amateurs, came to Tam O'Shanter to play in the All-American and the "World" championship tournaments held for each category. The pros played for the most purse money ever offered up to that time—an incredible $50,000 for winning the "World" event.

Sam Snead was of course one of the brightest stars in the golfing sky at the time, and as I think back I believe that even if you somehow didn't know of Sam's achievements you would have been able to tell by the way he walked, dressed, and above all swung his clubs. There was in his carriage and performance a remarkable combination of elegance and strength. He was Fred Astaire in a tuxedo dancing Ginger Rogers around a marble floor, as well as Charles Atlas getting back at the guys who had kicked sand in his face when he was a skinny kid with pimples. Sam Snead awakened in me a richer vision of athleticism. Playing games was not simply brute force. For a kid who wasn't all that big physically but had good form in sports, this was a nice thing to know.

Fascinated by the problem of how to hit a golf ball, I watched a myriad of swings at Tam O'Shanter during those two weeks in July and August. There was quite a variety in the days before the technology of video cameras and other outlets for swing technique information more or less homogenized the golf swing. There were all sorts of motions made, lots of moving parts with not all of them necessarily working in conjunction with the others. All of which made Sam Snead's golf swing that much more glorious to see. Very often over the years when I was practicing and playing, and the shots were not going as well as I liked, I would say, "I'm going to put my Sam swing on." I'm sure it didn't look like his, but it felt like it and that was enough. Things got a bit better after that.

Eventually I got into the journalism side of golf, which gave me opportunities to be around Sam on a different level, more up close. The first opportunity came when I became a writer on the television program *Shell's Wonderful World of Golf.* My first show as a new hire was the famous match Sam played against Ben Hogan, at the Houston Country Club in Texas. A powerful, frightening thunderstorm delayed the play for a couple of hours. Sam and Hogan, the producer, the director, and other staff people, including myself, hung out in the pro shop waiting for the weather to break. Hogan was sitting in a chair near the door, and Sam was standing nearby telling jokes—very dirty jokes—in one of which Sam used a banana to illustrate a certain aspect of the story. The thing about it was, there were women in the room—our script "girl," and another woman well known in golf who was officiating the match. I was amazed that Sam seemed to take no notice of these women as he told his pungent, explicit tales. Hogan smiled, guardedly; the women as I recall had blank stares; and I'm sure everyone felt uncomfortable. Everyone but Snead. Not yet experienced much in the world, and still a romantic idolater of sports heroes, I was taken aback and disappointed by Sam's performance in that pro shop. It was an awakening, a reality check, as the expression goes, that rubbed some of the allure off an icon.

Another picture of Sam came to me in Atlanta during a week of filming another match for the Shell show, this one between Sam and Julius Boros. Here I had an opportunity to play a round of golf with Sam, which was a coup in that he was well known for not wanting to play with amateurs, and also just because I could tee it up with a boyhood hero and one of the greatest golfers of all time. I was a single-digit golfer, so I didn't slow things up. But the highlight of the episode came when Sam asked me what club I hit on a par-three hole where I hit first and put my tee shot onto the green. My goodness, I thought to myself, I must not be too bad a player if the great Sam Snead thinks he can judge his club selection based on my game. But I discovered soon that Sam asked everybody what clubs they used, even high-handicap golfers. The discovery opened up the notion that this man who always seemed so invulnerable indeed had a certain lack of self-confidence.

In a word, he was becoming more a mere mortal. I liked that. It came home to me finally when I was putting together a book called *Gettin' to the Dance Floor: An Oral History of American Golf.* This was in the mid-1980s, when Sam was well past his playing days. The book contains reminiscences of various people who spent a lifetime in golf in one capacity or another, from tournament players to golf teachers to administrators of the game, all telling how and why they got into golf and describing their experiences in the game. When I contacted Sam to ask if he would like to be part of the book, he said sure. I was pleasantly surprised. I had thought he wouldn't be interested, especially since I didn't have a budget to pay him if he wanted some money for his contribution. I expected that, given his reputation as a tough guy with a buck. However, he never said a word about being paid.

I visited him in his house on the hill in Hot Springs, Virginia, and got another and deeper insight on the man. He spoke of his growing-up years, of his parents, and of his friends in ways that were far more intimate than I expected. Once and for all, I concluded that Sam Snead was not, or certainly not only, the hard-nosed and cranky cheapskate he had always been made out to be. Thus grew the germ of the idea to do a biography of Sam, for he was more than a mere giant in sports performance, he was a person who had lived a life inside and outside the arena and *was aware of both sides*. It took a few years to come around to doing that biography, but it has now come to pass, and the initial desire that drove me to do this book has been more than satisfied.

Sam may not have been the most worldly of men. Most of his life was lived within a relatively narrow ambit—golf, hunting and fishing, and women—but he explored them to the full. He had wonderful moments of great achievement in his public life, terrifically disappointing ones as well, and some very sad events in his private life. And he felt them all. He was a complex man, full of contradictions in the way he was perceived by those who didn't know him well, or at all and in how he tried to be perceived.

In that respect, one more thought. The ancient Greeks of the time of Plato and Aristotle had a worldview that held that nothing is perfect, or should be, and played out the thought in the construction of their great buildings, such as the Parthenon. There would purposely be an imperfection or two built in—one column a bit shorter than all the others, an ornament slightly deformed. Sam Snead exemplified that notion. He was quite a profane man. He peppered his conversation with four-letter words and could otherwise be crude in a social setting, the dirty jokes being the most obvious example. And yet, in his golf game generally and in the way he swung the club he was the essence of poetry in motion. Which for me makes him a more rounded human being. I hope that is what you take away from this biography.

INTRODUCTION

WHEN THIS BIOGRAPHY OF SAM SNEAD WAS FIRST published in a hardback edition in 2005, some people in the book-reviewing media asked why Snead? Perhaps some of those people were so young they didn't know who he was. That happens in our short-memory modern-day world, and those of us from a previous generation must somehow bear with such lack of knowledge. In any case, the reason for a biography of Sam Snead is self-explanatory when you consider that he was one of the best golfers to ever play the game and will, for all time, be in that category. It would be gross disrespect to not chronicle the life of so accomplished an athlete, especially in a world that is so taken with sports and its most accomplished players.

Not that there haven't been Snead life stories told. Most of them, though, have been in the form of autobiographies in which Snead dictated what would be told to the persons putting them together. It is my view these were only treatments, in the sense that only the aspects of Snead's life that he wished to talk of were aired, which is to say that a lot was left out. This is hardly uncommon among celebrated people who offer such books while they are still alive.

For example, Snead's only reference to his mentally disabled son were brief mentions to the effect that he was not always well. I don't believe Sam was ashamed of Terry's condition so much as it was so painful for him that he couldn't or didn't want to discuss it with anyone. My going into how Sam felt about and dealt with his second child is to give us a much richer perception of him as a human being.

As we know, great golfers or highly successful people in any line of work are much more than the sum of their accomplishments. The same idea was behind my including Sam's propensity for telling dirty jokes, and his womanizing. Some of his friends have said I was talking of all that just to titillate readers and to sell the book on those grounds. That was not at all the case. In terms of his joke-telling, I tried to put into a life-context just why he would sometimes tell them in settings that were by normal standards not proper—stories fit only for locker rooms were told at award dinners in chandeliered rooms with an audience dressed to the nines in tuxedos and long gowns. I really believe Sam was kind of getting some licks in at the monied, high-society people who vacationed at the Homestead Hotel, where Sam worked as a young man, and who he perceived were treating him as a second-class citizen.

As for his womanizing, I didn't try any deep analysis simply because I am not expert enough; I'm not sure anyone is. I got the sense at times that his attitude about sex was that of a teenager just feeling his oats, and that it never changed. Certainly his marriage, amazingly lifelong, had a role. The fact that his wife knew all along of his philandering says something about husband-wife relationships being even more complicated than generally understood. And, too, when a traveling man is away from home as much as Snead was, well, one must relieve himself of certain pressures. And when you are famous and not at all bad looking, it is very easy to find the required companionship. He was by no means alone in the category.

Finally, while the hardcover edition of this biography was handsomely produced, my feeling was that it had the character of a so-called tabletop volume, the kind of book that people casually browse, interested mainly in the pictures. I meant the book to be read, with the pictures a kind of bonus. With this edition I expect more people will take the book and Sam Snead more seriously.

1

==

THE SNEADS
OF VIRGINIA

SAM SNEAD'S DAZZLING DEBUT ON THE AMERICAN GOLF stage, in 1937, seemed like an alien landing. Snead? Who's he? The name was new, but only to golf. In various spellings, the name Snead, which means a clearing or a piece of land, goes back at least to thirteenth-century England. It is found in English place names such as Sneaton and Halsnead, and a township in Staffordshire is named Sneyd. A man named Snod lived in Suffolk in 1273; Robert del Sned and Agnes Sned lived in Worcestershire in 1275; Robert Snede was in Worcestershire and John Snode in Suffolk in 1327. William Sneade and John Sneade are listed in the Oxford University Register. There were Sneads (and Sneeds) in Virginia before the American Revolution. Virginia land records show a John Snede holding land in Elizabeth City prior to 1635. A Samuel Snead obtained a two hundred–acre land grant in James City County in 1635, and another Samuel Snead held land in York County prior to 1651. Around 1666, Charles Snead held a total of 1,939 acres in Old Rappahannock County. Three men named Snead or Snede or Sneyd were officers in the American Revolutionary Army.

The first Sneads most closely related to the Sam Snead who would become one of the greatest golfers of all time settled in Virginia during the pre–American Revolution years. Sam's great-grandfather, Richard, came over from England in the mid-1770s and received a land grant of some sixty acres in Bath County that has been in the family ever since. It is now called Olde Snead Links. It is about three miles from the village of Hot Springs, in an area called Ashwood. It is where Sam Snead spent his summers for the last twenty-five years of his life, and where he is buried.

Sam's grandfather and grandmother had a number of children, among them George and Harry. Harry Snead was Sam's father. He married Laura Dudley, and they had six children, Lyle, Homer, Janet, Jess, Welford, and Sam, in that order. George and Harry owned the Snead farm but did not work it very successfully, and they leased it out while retaining ownership. George Snead moved to California, and Harry moved his family into a six-room house about two miles from the farm and about the same distance from the Cascades Golf Course, where Sam had his first grounding in the game of golf. In the six-room house (still standing and lived in) Harry and Laura Snead raised the children. It was a tight squeeze as the children grew, if only because almost all of them were big. The children shared rooms and beds. Sam shared a bed with his sister, who was nine years older, and he kept his clothes in a box beneath the bed.

Sam liked to tell the press that he grew up poor. The truth depends on how that is defined. Certainly there was no extra money to go around. From the time he was nine years old Sam had to earn his own money for clothes and whatnot. Christmas was not a bountiful gift-giving holiday. Sam would say the best he ever did was a sled his father made for him; usually it was a few coins left under the breakfast plate on Christmas morning, and some years a pair of socks or an orange. It left Sam with a bad taste for Christmas, and as an adult he never celebrated the holiday. But there was always a roof over the Sneads' heads, and always food on the table. The only thing that Sam ever did to peeve his sister was when he told the world he often had to shoot squirrels so the family had something to eat. That was not so. They had a cow for milk and butter, a garden for vegetables, some chickens for eggs. The Snead family got by, was never without.

To support the family, Harry worked for the Homestead Hotel, in Hot Springs. It is one of the oldest resorts in the country, dating back to 1766. The hotel dominates the village (which to this day has a population of around three hundred), not only as the principal if not the sole source of work for the locals but by its very size. It is a massive, curving red brick building in the Georgian architectural style, featuring a high clock tower that pokes in lordly eminence above the trees and the village just below.

Harry Snead was an "engineer," as Sam liked to put it. He worked in the hotel powerhouse as an all-around handyman. He shoveled coal mainly, and fixed things and served on the hotel's firefighting crew. Harry Snead was a very quiet, religious man who for thirty-two years almost never missed a Sunday in church. He was fastidious, and had an odd tic: he hated having anyone touch his head. He told the barber to do very little, and to do it as fast as he could. Sylvia Snead, Sam's sister-in-law via Jesse, remembered once running her hand in fun over the top of Harry's head. "He jumped up and ran off. I laughed, but Jesse told me that if it had been anyone else but me he would have hit me."

Every morning of the week Harry Snead dressed in a three-piece suit and walked some three miles to work. When he arrived he changed into his coveralls and shoveled coal, and did other chores. At day's end he took a shower, put his suit back on, and walked home. Sam remembered a piece of advice his father gave him: "Son, if your fingernails are clean and your shoes are polished you can get by with the rest." Indeed, from his first days in the public eye, Sam was noted as a smart dresser. He would be best known for his straw hat with a wide, colorful band, but his slacks, shirts, sweaters, and sport jackets were always perfectly fitted, tastefully color-coordinated, and of the best quality. He carried clothes well on his trim, muscular body. His baldness, which became prominent in his middle thirties, was always a source of irritation to him. He tried wigs now and then, and when wearing them he liked to be called John, but they were never success-ful. One year he showed up at the Masters and walked into a room full of fellow players, including Jimmy Demaret, a wit and sharp needler. When Sam asked Demaret how he liked his "rug," Demaret said, "Sam, you've taken a million dollars out of this game and all you can afford is a second-class head of hair." Sam ripped off the wig and stormed off.

Interestingly, as a boy, Sam Snead, who once held the record for the biggest bonefish ever caught, who would shoot bears in Alaska, who hit a golf ball harder and farther than anybody, learned tailoring skills. He could alter the waist and length of his trousers, and turn the frayed collar of a coat. Sam Snead was a man of many more parts than the public ever knew about.

Laura Snead was a woman who ran her family with a firm hand. What she said to her children went; there was no questioning Laura's Law. Sam would say that he only knew his mother as an old woman, which was understandable in that she was forty-seven when she gave birth to him, but he was deeply devoted to her. Long after she had died, he spoke of her often and with no little reverence. Quoted in this writer's 1986 book *Gettin' to the Dance Floor: An Oral History of American*

Golf, Sam said, "I'd like to have had all my characteristics and character from my mother [as compared with his "touchy" father]. She was one of the few people I ever knew who had front sight as well as hindsight. We never went to my dad for anything. We always went to my mother." One of the theories as to why Sam played so well in the Greensboro Open (he won it eight times) held that it was the last stop on the winter tour, and he was exhilarated at knowing that an hour or so after he played the last hole he would be home to see his mother.

A fundamental Snead family characteristic was physical size and strength. A recollection of any Snead family member by another almost invariably begins with how big and strong he or she was, followed by evidence. First and foremost was the legendary John Snead, Sam's great uncle, who stood seven feet, nine inches tall, weighed 360 pounds, and wore a size 28 shoe. Incredible? Mythical? Jack Snead, Sam's eldest son, went to the Bath County courthouse once to verify the figures. "They were what they were said to be. What's more, he was perfectly proportioned," said Jack. "He didn't have the disease called gigantism. There is a story about him that when people would clear a pasture and put a split-rail fence around it that was made up of eleven-foot long rails of chestnut, a stout farmer could carry two of those rails over each shoulder. But then here comes Uncle John out of the woods with six over each shoulder. Twelve altogether!" Perhaps.

Harry Snead, though not particularly muscular, had big hands and powerful arms. Sam relayed a story about his father's strength: "We had a firemen's team and we'd pull this heavy reel of hose off wheels that were six feet high. Ten guys. We'd run 125 yards pulling that hose and hook it up to a hydrant, put a nozzle on it, and have water coming out in twenty seconds. My dad would run down there with the team when he was seventy years old." Laura Snead was a tall, stockily built woman who could throw a hundred-pound sack of flour up onto a rack. Her daughter, Janet, who stood close to six feet tall, could do the same. Jesse Snead was the biggest of them all, at six feet two, 250 pounds. "They always talked about how strong Sam was," said Jesse Carlyle (J. C.) Snead, Sam's nephew through Jesse and Sylvia, "and he was. But my dad could have pinched his head off." Sneads talk like that.

Homer Snead, who was Sam's idol growing up, was a big man with considerable athletic ability. That ability was not realized because he had to help support the family. He may also have been a bit lazy. Homer could hit a golf ball farther than his kid brother, albeit with nothing like the same fine form and balance—"Homer just about fell off his feet when he hit it," said Bobby Fry, a golf pro from Hot Springs who knew the Sneads well. "He took divots as big as beaver pelts." Homer was a good boxer who might have done something in the ring, but one day when he was scheduled to fight an especially tough, seasoned pro he took the advice to skip the opportunity to get badly beaten up.

Welford, who disliked his given name and went by Pete all his life, was about Sam's size, close to six feet and solidly built. Lyle was the least hale of the Snead boys. He worked as a barber, and, a heavy cigarette smoker, died at the age of sixty-eight of emphysema. Sam, who never smoked and would not tolerate anyone smoking in any closed room in which he was present, put Lyle's death in the prosaic terms of his culture: "The poor devil choked to death."

Sam, because of his celebrity, would become the apotheosis of the Snead family's physicality and pride of body. His most famous demonstration of those qualities was to stand in a doorway and, with one foot flat to the floor, kick the top of the door jamb with the other. It was (pun intended) the kick-off of every Masters Champions dinner. When Sam came into the doorway and did his high kick, Hogan, Nelson, Burke, Ford, Palmer, and all the others knew it was time to dine.

Dave Stockton remembered an even more amazing exhibition of Sam's specialty. It was at a Greensboro Open, in the early 1970s, when Sam was in his late fifties. Stockton and other players were in a dining area adjacent to the locker room when they heard a crashing noise they identified, correctly, as someone kicking in a locker door. It was Sam, angry over a poor round. When he came to the dining area he stopped in the doorway, gripped the side door jambs, turned himself upside down, and kicked in the ceiling. "It was unbelievable," said Stockton. "We all started laughing and applauding, and Sam, when he straightened himself up again, had this proud smile on his face."

Bill Campbell is a West Virginian with one of the best lifetime records in American amateur golf, a former president of the United States Golf Association, and a lifelong friend of Sam. He recalled a time in 1938 when he got a firsthand taste of Sam's physical prowess. "We were in Wheeling for the Virginia State Open. I was fifteen, eleven years Sam's junior, and we shared a room in the McClure Hotel. One morning before we left for the course Sam asked me how many push-ups I could do. I said I didn't know, and he prompted me to give it a try. I did maybe ten, which was a mistake because my arms went wobbly for the rest of the day. Then Sam got down on his fingertips and bounced up and down like a cat; he must have done fifty, maybe a hundred. He was so strong. You didn't see it in his golf swing, because it was so fluid."

Of the five Snead boys, four played golf with varying degrees of proficiency. (Sister Janet didn't; she married early and raised six children in Waynesboro, Virginia.) Homer was a casual player, although it didn't take much persuading to get him out for a round. Jesse, who worked most of his life for the Homestead Hotel, could shoot in the 70s. Pete was the only other Snead boy to become a golf professional. He held the head professional's job at the Pittsburgh Field Club for nearly fifty years. He was giving lessons at the club well into his nineties, before a stroke stopped him. Pete had a rather nervous disposition and a short, quick golf swing to match. He did, however, share one of his younger brother's predilections. One winter Pete played the pro tour, although with not much distinction, the probable reason becoming clear when Sam made the circuit the following season. He was regularly approached by young, attractive women who Sam thought at first were interested in him. But they all asked where his brother was. Pete had a way with the ladies, too, but in his case it apparently hurt his golf.

Pete, by the way, was not the only Snead boy dissatisfied with his moniker. Jesse's middle name was James, but he never used it. He didn't like the connection to the famous outlaw. Jesse J. would do, thank you. Sam wanted to be called Jack, a diminution of his middle name, but his mother wouldn't permit it, and that was that. His best friend, Johnny Bulla, made up for it by calling him Jackson most of the time. Jackson, by the way, was in honor of Stonewall Jackson, the famed Confederate general and a native Virginian, whom Sam's grandfather knew.

Size and strength were central points of pride among the Sneads, but there were other dimensions to the clan. Pete developed a sideline as an expert furniture maker. Homer, who was the only one to go beyond high school—he attended a technical school in Pittsburgh—had an innate genius for electronics, and was inventive in that and other areas. During World War II he worked on electrical problems for the U.S. Navy, at Norfolk, Virginia.

When the radio was first introduced in the United States, Homer studied manuals and made a radio of his own that might have made him a fortune. In typical Snead fashion, Homer's manmade radio was oversized—nine feet long, weighing over three hundred pounds, and with a speaker nine feet in diameter. With it Homer could pull in broadcasts from stations around the country, and on one occasion he picked up the radio account of the famous "long-count" Jack Dempsey–Gene Tunney heavyweight championship fight. He hung his speaker in a tree on one of the Homestead golf courses (the hotel owned three, the only ones in town). The speaker was so powerful, legend has it, that people could hear the punch-by-punch three miles away.

Another time, in the day when high-society easterners such as the Vanderbilts, Whitneys, and Astors regularly took the waters at the Homestead (as had Thomas Jefferson some years earlier), a group of them were anxious to hear a special sporting event that was being broadcast. They were told Homer Snead had the only radio in town, and off went the nobs to Ashwood. One of the visitors took particular interest in Homer's radio, on which he had fitted the tubes in the back with metal shields that kept static electricity from jumping from one tube to the other. This eliminated a popping noise that was common in the radios of the time. The gentleman—J. C. Snead speculates it might have been David Sarnoff, the powerful president of RCA and the National Broadcasting System—asked Homer how he figured out the static bypass. Homer explained it, and the gentleman allegedly took the idea back to New York and incorporated it into RCA-produced radios. Homer, of course, got not a dime for it.

Homer also invented a photoelectric dimmer for cars that would make lights on high beam automatically go to low beam when a car approached from the opposite direction. He created a CB radio, and a hydraulic clutch for automobiles and trucks. He never tried to patent any of his inventions, however, or capitalize on his ideas. It was not his way.

For a number of years Homer ran a radio repair shop in Waynesboro, Virginia. He went into television repair when the "tube" came out, and ended up operating a driving range in Fort Lauderdale, Florida.

Just about all the Sneads made music, and the Dudleys, too. Laura Snead played guitar and had a brother who played organ, trumpet, and guitar, and a sister who weighed in at over two hundred pounds and sang opera. Harry Snead played trumpet, Jesse the bass, and Pete the saxophone. All three, and also Ed Dudley, Sam's uncle, made some extra money sitting in when needed with the dance band at Homestead soirees. "They all played by ear, couldn't read a note," said J. C. Snead, "but they were good enough to fill in with the professionals. They played stuff like 'Stardust,' 'Indian Summer.' Swing music, no hillbilly or mountain music. My dad always said bluegrass and hillbilly music sounded like a barrelful of rocks rolling down a hill."

Sam played banjo and trumpet, and sang a nice second tenor. As a teenager he saved up for three years to buy a Gibson guitar that today is worth quite a lot of money; it's on display at the Greenbrier Hotel, along with other artifacts of his. "Dad relaxed at home playing a trumpet," Jack Snead recalled. "He used a mute and got in the back of a closet so he wouldn't disturb Mom."

It is not uncommon for people with musical ability who play golf to have rhythmic swings and good form. Among show people, Bing Crosby was a good example. Dean Martin and Perry Como were two others. John Williams, the composer of award-winning movie scores, has classic golf form and a well-cadenced swing. So it comes as no surprise that when Sam Snead swung a golf club it was like a conductor directing Debussy, or a Strauss waltz. Sam not only enjoyed music for its own sake, he used it as a kind of metronome for his golf. He whistled and hummed a lot when playing and practicing, often a waltz tune but also melodies out of the popular American songbook of the 1930s and '40s—"Stardust," "Sentimental Journey"—and the recordings of swing orchestras such as Glenn Miller's.

But there was another factor that shaped Sam's exquisite tempo. When he first began to play golf he had no money for clubs and fashioned his first ones from broken buggy whips given to him by a friend who worked in a stable, a black man named Frank Underwood who was called Stetson (and who also happened to play a French harp). Uncle Ed Dudley gave Sam some old Tom Stewart ironheads that he attached to the buggy whips. A few of these clubs are on display at the World Golf Hall of Fame, in St. Augustine, Florida. To hit a ball with a shaft as flexible as a buggy whip and carrying a solid metal head weighing a quarter of a pound, one cannot rush the swing. Do so and the ball will probably be missed, for one thing, and for another the clubhead might bean you or break a knee. You have to "wait on it," as the saying goes in golf, meaning let the clubhead lag behind the hands. There is currently a training device with a similarly soft "spaghetti" shaft and a driverhead attached that golfers with tempo problems use to slow themselves down. By accident, eleven-year-old Sam Snead was about a half century ahead of the learning curve. If you can master hitting the ball with a spaghetti shaft, you will hit the ball ten to fifteen yards farther with what seems like a slower swing. Which is also why Sam's enormous power was masked. In golf pro parlance he was a soft hitter, but it only looked that way.

Like all kids from the working class in the early days of American golf, Sam Snead was introduced to the game through caddieing. The lure at first was not the game so much as a means by which a youngster could make some money. He was seven when he first started "looping." However, as it also often happens, he was attracted to playing the game. With knob-headed branches taken from swamp maple trees he made his first swings, hitting stones, acorns, found golf balls.

Sam was a born athlete, and he immediately displayed talent for golf. But as he went through high school he got into other sports that were more accessible. Golf was very much a rich man's game in Hot Springs; it was played only at the Homestead, its courses reserved for hotel guests. There were no public courses, and young Sam would sneak onto the hotel's courses in late afternoon, or play a very hilly, unkempt one called The Goat that hotel guests rarely if ever played. Sam played football, basketball, and baseball. He also ran the 100-yard dash in 10 seconds.

Sam might also have been a high jumper. Sylvia Snead, who married into the family when Sam was still in high school, recalled how her teenage brother-in-law used to jump a board fence around the house. "I told him, Sam, you're going to catch your toe on that top rail and fall and kill yourself. He didn't listen." It was a predilection Sam never seems to have lost. Bob Goalby remembered watching Sam during a practice round at the Masters tournament. "He came off the second green and jumped the gallery rope, clicked his heels while in the air, landed on the other side. I was lucky I didn't trip just stepping over it."

His high school coach, Harold Bell, spoke of Sam's athletic ability once, saying that he was a fast and shifty runner in football, that he was a good baseball pitcher who didn't learn to control his stuff until he was a junior but then showed a good drop and an assortment of curveballs, and that he had a good eye for shooting the basketball, which was his best game.

He also did some boxing. One day, a Golden Gloves fighter came through Hot Springs and asked around for someone to give him a few rounds of workout. Sam got in the ring and knocked the fellow out in round two. After his high school days and before he got into golf, Sam would be one of the boys who boxed on Friday nights in Hot Springs. The fights were put on for the folks staying at the Homestead. He got fifty dollars a fight, win or lose. Sam would be a fight fan for all his days, and he once had a small interest in the featherweight champion Sandy Saddler. He also had a larger interest in a heavyweight fighter who he thought might go somewhere, but he was warned to not get into the fight game on that level because it was controlled by mobsters and might bring him trouble he didn't need. One of Sam's favorite pastimes for the rest of his life was watching the fights on television. He once failed to appear at a state dinner given by the King of Morocco, staying in his room instead to watch the fights on television. He did the same thing many times with less regal hosts.

Sam was offered athletic scholarships to a couple of Virginia colleges, but coach Bell and he talked it over and decided otherwise. "Coach Bell thought that by the time I spent four years in golf I'd be farther ahead than if I went to college." Sam recalled (in *Gettin' to the Dance Floor*), "I wanted to be an athlete." And so he became one.

Obviously, Sam had shown more than a little talent for golf by that time, when he was in his mid-teens. But in the backwoods of rural Virginia in the 1920s there were no junior golf programs, nor much of an amateur tournament circuit a young fellow like him could afford to play. So as a teenager he had very limited tournament experience. Two events, to be exact. Harold Bell took Sam to play in the Virginia Interscholastic High School championship in his junior and senior years. His best finish was eighth, but, displaying the power that would be a major mark of his game in the years ahead, he won the driving contest both times.

To keep himself in clothes and spending money, Sam caddied and worked at the drugstore in Hot Springs as a soda jerk and handyman. When the drugstore closed, he went across the street and cleaned up his uncle Ed's restaurant. Then he got lucky. During the summer when he was a senior in high school, Sam got a job in the pro shop at the Homestead. Here he learned to assemble hickory-shafted golf clubs. It was effectively his start as a golf professional, and as something of a craftsman to boot.

In those days before the steel shaft was introduced, the hickory shafts all came in raw form with the same taper and length. They had to be modified, and Sam learned to cut the shafts to the length required—shortest for the niblick or 9-iron, and graduating up to the longest for the driver—and then to taper them with a pocket knife, shards of glass, and sandpaper. The trick was to make each shaft in a set have the same flexibility. Not an easy job. Each piece of wood had slightly different characteristics in grain and density. And there was, of course, the human element. Every shaft maker had a slightly different touch.

From this work Sam developed a true feel for clubs—their weight, balance, flexibility—that made him an especially adept testing machine for the Wilson Sporting Goods Company, whose golf equipment he played and endorsed for almost his entire career. When the company came out with a new model of club, they brought it to Sam out on the tour to get his reaction and input. Many of the tour pros did this for their equipment companies, but Sam's examination, given the exceptional consistency of his ball striking and his background in shaft making, made him the Father Superior of human test benches.

Then he got even luckier. On a quiet morning in the summer of 1930, a woman guest at the hotel came by seeking a golf lesson. Sam notified her that the two teaching pros were out playing, and she asked if he could do it. Sam tells the rest, in his inimitable style (this story also appeared in *Gettin' to the Dance Floor*):

"I sort of hummed and hawed and a guy named Keeser, who was the starter, said, 'Go ahead, I'll look out for you.' I didn't know whether she should swing over or under her bosom, but I knew a few tricks, like laying out the clubs for alignment, and I worked her. Boy, she was sweating after I got through with her.

"After the lesson was over she said, 'Young man, you should have a club of your own.' I said I was working on it and that I hoped to some day. Well, she was the right type of person. She spoke to the manager of the hotel and said he had a kid down there that knows his business. Two days later the athletic director, Toby Hanson, said to me, 'Come upstairs, I want to talk to you.' I thought maybe I'd done something wrong or somebody was laying something on me, but he said, 'How'd you like to go over to the Cascades course as a pro?' There hadn't been anybody over there since the Crash in '29. He said I'd get whatever I could in lessons, and a glass of milk and a sandwich for lunch. So I went over there. Of course, now I had a chance to practice, and I beat sod. Oh, I beat sod. They said, 'Hey you're beating all the grass off.' I broke the course record twice the first two weeks on the job. But that was a rough year, because people weren't traveling much. I would rent my clubs out for a buck and a half—half of them, so I'd have the other half if somebody came along who wanted to play a little game."

An insidious psychology takes hold of some people when there comes among them a person with special talent. Those not as gifted are prone to resentment or jealousy, and they try to even things up when they have the chance. Sam Snead encountered this attitude as soon as it was clear he was at least one step above the ordinary as a golfer. The envious slights started early on, and because he was still at a time in his life when first experiences take a strong hold and shape an attitude, he would for the rest of his days be suspicious and distrustful of people.

One such instance of backbiting occurred when he first began working at the Homestead. Sam did not own a proper set of clubs at first, and he began to put a set together one at a time. When he had enough for one club he went to the pro from whom he bought them, Freddie Gleims, who charged Sam five dollars for each club. That was a fair bit of money in the Depression 1930s. The point is, it was the same price the guests at the hotel, people of wealth, paid. There has always been a code among people in the golf business that those in the fraternity, fellow pros, pay the "pro price"—wholesale—for equipment they buy. Gleims broke the code in Sam's case, and he would on at least two other occasions help to shape Sam's wary response to the world at large.

The first time Sam went to play in the Miami Open, in 1935, he used a 2-wood that belonged to Gleims. He used it as his driver, and it suited him very well. He won $150 in the tournament, and afterward Gleims told Sam he needed to have his 2-wood back. "I told him I was going over to Nassau to play, but he said he had to have the club," as Sam recalled (in *Gettin' to the Dance Floor*). "So I don't have a club to play with, and have to go back home. Gleims leaves for Nassau, and I go look in the locker he was using. I just wanted to see if that club wasn't there. Well, it was there. Gleims didn't take it to Nassau; he just didn't want me to go."

The most egregious hoodwink Gleims played on Sam came during the 1935 Cascades Open, played at and sponsored by the Homestead. In this case, however, Gleims was the agent of a higher authority. Johnny Farrell, the 1928 U.S. Open champion, who participated in the tournament, told his son Billy, many years later, that the Homestead people did not want to let Sam play in the event in the first place, apparently because they feared he might win. The field consisted of a good number of nationally known golfers, including stars such as Bobby Cruickshank and future U.S. Open winners Lawson Little and Billy Burke. When they heard that the young Snead fellow was being blacklisted, the stars told the sponsor they would not play if he wasn't allowed in. Sam played, and sure enough he shot a first-round 63. After three rounds he led the field. That's when the chicanery was put in motion. When the president of the Homestead, Fay Ingalls, came to his office the morning of the fourth and final round and learned Sam was the leader, he told Gleims that it wouldn't do for that boy to win. He wanted the winner to be someone who was well known, so the hotel got more publicity. Ingalls told Gleims to mess Sam up, somehow, so he didn't win.

On the first tee, Gleims took Sam aside and asked him how he expected to be a pro with his right elbow coming out the way it did on his backswing. It was a classic "gotcha" in golf gamesmanship. Get someone thinking about his swing mechanics in a way that provokes a loss of self-confidence or just too much thinking. Sam was got. There is a photograph of him going down the first fairway with Burke and Farrell moments after the Gleims "tip." He has a tight-lipped scowl on his face, a reflection of the anger he felt knowing that Gleims was trying to undo him. Coach Bell had counseled Sam about dealing with temper, telling him that when you give in to it you lose control, that you have to channel your anger and stay cool mad. But he wasn't able to do it this time. On the second hole, not because he "fixed" his right elbow but because he was angry at Gleims, Sam hooked his tee shot high up into the trees. He took an eight on the hole, shot an 80, and finished third. Burke won. Sam never forgot the incident, and it made him wary the rest of his life of "help" from others with his swing, business decisions, medical issues, just about everything but women.

The episode would also, in this writer's view, echo down through the rest of Sam's life in his response to people of wealth and position. Once he rose in the world of golf and became a celebrity, Sam did not kowtow to people of social rank. When appearing at golf outings or other events at which "important" people were present, if on arrival he first ran into a caddie he knew or an assistant professional or other working-class types, that's who he spoke with first, and for as long as it took. The bigshots could wait. He once offered some explicit golf instruction to President Eisenhower. "Mister Ike," he said, "at address you need to stick your ass out." A Secret Service agent immediately came beside Sam and whispered to him that he couldn't talk like that to the President of the United States. To which Sam replied, "Why not, he's got one, hasn't he?"

Sam's play in the 1935 Cascades Open had a positive side, however—a career-changing one. Not long after finishing the last round, Sam was approached by Freddie Martin, the golf manager at the Greenbrier Hotel, who offered him a job. The Greenbrier, which was founded in 1904 in White Sulphur Springs, West Virginia, about an hour's drive from Hot Springs, had become a fierce business rival of the Homestead. Martin told Sam that if he ever wanted to go to work at the Greenbrier to just let him know. Sam asked what was in it for him, and was told $45 a month, room and board, and half his lessons. Sam said he'd be there the next day. And he was.

Although at the time the Homestead was not paying Sam much more than when he started out—his lessons and a bit of lunch—Fay Ingalls was unhappy with Sam for making this move. Ingalls said he should have been given a chance to make a counteroffer. But after what had happened on the morning of the last round of the Cascades Open, Sam understandably felt no obligation to do that. His connection with the Greenbrier would have a couple of gaps, including one bitter breakup, but essentially Sam represented the resort for the rest of his life. Yet, while Sam would have rooms in which to live when at the Greenbrier, he always maintained his family home in Hot Springs. He was in many respects a true homeboy.

On the surface it would seem a wonder that a fellow like Sam Snead, from such a small and relatively isolated back mountain area of Virginia, should emerge and become a world-famous celebrity. But it wasn't all back mountain. Despite some unhappy events there, Sam was fortunate to work at the Homestead Hotel. If it was not in Hot Springs but in South Carolina, say, or Florida, when young Sam was growing up, golf might never have heard of him. Nor he of golf. Sam developed a certain animosity toward the monied, privileged class that vacationed at the resort, but those people were the vent that opened up to him the outside world. Indeed, they introduced him to it. The American aristocracy (or plutocracy) was a major factor in his career. For one thing, they brought a certain worldly sophistication to his attention, no matter that he didn't seem to pick up a lot of it. Surely Sam's taste in clothes was affected. But beyond that, the moneyed class that came to the Homestead always had an eye out for fresh talent, for people out of the ordinary whom they might use for their own entertainment, or devices, or for the simple satisfaction of bringing something or someone exceptional out into the world at large. Whatever the motive, this was often a good thing for the discovered talent. And so it was for Sam.

The grandees who visited the Homestead in the 1920s and '30s discovered an untutored young fellow named Snead who could hit the golf ball a mile, had the game to go with it—he was shooting some phenomenally low scores—and, most intriguingly, did it all with an uncommon grace of movement. They were (and are) a horsy crowd—owners, breeders, racers of thoroughbreds—and saw in Sam a War Admiral, albeit with a Seabiscuit personality that made him all the more fascinating. And, a good bet.

The racing metaphor is not arbitrary. Sam often talked with his friend, Lew Keller, of an episode that highlights its relevance. While Sam was still associated with the Homestead, in 1935, two New Yorkers who were guests at the hotel saw him play. They were sporting types who savored pulling off a betting coup. With that in mind, the two gentlemen arranged for Sam to go up to New York to play a money match against a quality amateur who liked playing for big stakes. The amateur's name was T. (for Thomas) Suffern Tailer—Tommy, to his friends. Tommy Tailer came from old money. He had a home in Newport, Rhode Island, where the likes of the Vanderbilts, Morgans, Astors, and Belmonts kept thirty-five-room summer "cottages," and he wintered in Palm Beach, where he was a member of that city's gilded social whirl. Tailer was no dillettante at golf. He competed in the 1934, '37, and '38 U.S. Amateur championships, and in the 1938 and '40 Masters. And, of course, he won regional and state amateur championships.

Sam's backers paid his travel expenses, which included Sam's very first train ride. The match was played at the exclusive Meadowbrook Club, on Long Island. Sam won the match—not handily, but he won. At that, Tailer wanted another go, and got it the next day. He played well, and through the first ten or eleven holes he held a slim lead. Sam's backers got nervous, but he reassured them that he would win. It was a squeaker, but he came through. When it was over his backers gave Sam $10,000 in cash. He would later learn that the first match was for $50,000, the second for $100,000. Sam received a rather small percentage of the total, but he put up nothing of his own, and since it was in the depths of the Great Depression Sam didn't mind. He took the train back to Virginia carrying, no doubt, more money than he had ever seen at once or even in segments. It was a bundle that helped him get started on the pro tour.

Sam's rise to golfing prominence was remarkably fast given how little top-drawer, or even lower-drawer, competitive experience he had had when he joined the game's big league. In his very first outing against top professionals, the 1935 Cascade Open, he finished third despite the Ingalls/Gleims conspiracy. In 1936, he won the West Virginia Closed Professional tournament, which sounds local but involved defeating Harry Cooper in a playoff; Cooper was one of the stars of the pro tournament circuit. Later that same year Sam made his first real stab at the pro tour, entering the Miami Open, where he won $300 for a high finish. The following week, in Nassau, he again finished in the money. With those two performances he began thinking seriously about making the winter pro tour, which traditionally started the first week in January with the Los Angeles Open.

In Nassau, Sam asked Henry Picard and Craig Wood, two of the best players in American golf, if they thought he had a chance to make good out West. Picard reminded Sam that the prize-money list was short—only sixteen places, usually—with only the top three or four places yielding enough to make expenses. Wood, who was a patron saint of golf professionals, told Sam that if he ran out of money out there he would have some for him to get back home. It was the same offer Picard made to Ben Hogan a year or so later, offering the peace of mind Hogan needed to continue on the circuit when he was having great trouble with his game. Sam, too, felt more comfortable after Wood's offer. Finally, through Picard, Sam had signed an endorsement contract with the Dunlop

Tire and Rubber Company, which also made golf equipment. It brought him $500 a year, a set of clubs, and a dozen balls a month. Sam also had some of the money left from his big-money match on Long Island. So in all he wasn't hurting quite as badly as he would make out when telling his life story in the years to come. He said he went west with only $300 in his pocket, but Sam liked to talk poorer than he actually was. It was part of his personal monologue, his structured-for-the-public persona, and a defense against rogue borrowers.

And so, in January of 1937, Sam went west to try his luck on the pro tour. How to get out there? Sam didn't have a car of his own that could make such a trip. A friend named Leo Walper offered a ride, for half the gas and oil. But Walper was pulling a trailer, and Sam figured that would not only slow the trip but cost too much in gas. Then along came Johnny Bulla, who said he'd go. Sam had become friendly with Bulla while in Florida and Nassau. It was a friendship that lasted a lifetime and was as close as any Sam would ever have with another touring pro. Sam once said he thought as much of Boo-Boo, as he nicknamed him, as he did his brothers.

Bulla didn't go to college, but he was one of the more intellectually oriented pros of his time. Sam Snead was not a book reader, nor a considerer of philosophical thoughts other than the homespun variety, but he found in Bulla someone to whom he could open up his heart and mind. He might not have developed such a relationship with Bulla at that time if Bulla had not been a high-quality golfer. Sam often used that as a measure of someone's merit as a human being.

Bulla was indeed an interesting man. He grew up in Burlington, North Carolina, the son of a Quaker minister who strongly opposed his son's interest in golf. But Bulla persisted, and finally he went out into the world as a golf professional. He was born ambidextrous and preferred to play golf left-handed, but was firmly told he couldn't. The ancient superstition still prevailed that left-handedness was on the side of the devil. Bulla was convinced that if he had played left-handed from the beginning (he didn't play a southpaw round until he was forty years old) he would have been far more successful on the tour. As it was, he was good enough as a right-hander to win a Los Angeles Open, take two seconds in the British Open, lead the 1939 U.S. Open after three rounds, and otherwise become one of the better players on the pro tour in the 1930s and '40s. He also learned to fly, was a pilot for Eastern Airlines at one time, and then owned his own DC-6 passenger plane and for a fare flew tour pros around the tournament circuit.

Off went Sam and Boo-Boo to California in Bulla's 1936 Ford. In Greensboro, they picked up a young fellow Bulla knew was going to California to play college football. He agreed to pay half the gas and oil, which reduced Sam's and Boo-Boo's expenses by half. They were on a roll. Sam's uncle George, who had moved out to California, put Sam and Bulla up in his house in Los Angeles, another savings, although the two buddies had to sleep in the same bed. Tumultuously, as Sam recalled: "That sonofabuck [Bulla] could go to sleep like you cut off a light. He'd run his hand over his nose twice, pull the covers over him, and, bam, gone. Now, six o'clock in the morning, ping, he walks on his heels to the bathroom and shakes the building. John weighed about 235. Then he'd come run jump on the bed and we'd begin to wrestle. We tore up more rooms that way."

On the trip west Sam made Bulla an offer to split their tournament winnings. Bulla was not interested. He didn't think Sam was going to do that well, and was certain he himself was going to knock 'em dead. It was one of the poorer decisions Bulla ever made. During the days leading up to the start of the 1937 Los Angeles Open, Sam acquired two clubs that helped him get off to his exceptionally fast start as a touring pro. On the practice range one morning in Los Angeles he met Henry Picard, who had a lot of extra clubs he was trying out. One was an Izett driver that Sam took in hand and liked immediately. Picard told Sam to hit a few with it. After only a couple he said, "God, this is good." Picard told him it was his. Sam was elated. "See, one trouble I was having was with my driving," Sam said (as quoted in *Gettin' to the Dance Floor*). "I had a whippy-shafted driver I couldn't control. The driver I got from Picard had a stiff shaft, and my driving improved forty percent right there."

A few minutes later he went up to the practice putting green, where Leo Walper was practicing. Walper asked Sam if he wanted to putt for a quarter a hole. Sam didn't have a putter at hand, and took an extra one Walper had in his bag. It was a model of the "Calamity Jane" Bobby Jones used to win all his championships. Sam made three aces in a row against Walper, who then decided he'd had enough. He asked Sam if he wanted to buy the putter, for $3.50. Sam couldn't get the money out of his pocket fast enough. He was elated. Not long afterward he saw Bulla and told him he now had the two most important clubs in the bag, driver and putter, and that he was very confident of his chances. Bulla was not impressed and offered to play Sam for five dollars in every tournament, low total wins. Sam offered to double the bet. Bulla said five was enough. This time he made a good decision. Sam won $600 in the 1937 Los Angeles Open. The following week he won the Oakland Open, and a week later he won the inaugural Bing Crosby Pro-Am. At the far end of the winter tour Sam won the Miami and Nassau Opens. And in the summer of 1937 he won the St. Paul Open. In all, he had five victories, three seconds, and five thirds, and was the second-biggest money winner of the year not counting the five-spots he took off Bulla.

No golfer, including Tiger Woods, has ever made such a dynamic debut in major-league professional tournament golf. Here was a twenty-five-year-old fellow whose ability was known only among some folks in the Virginias and at a few points along the East Coast, who had no amateur record, and yet made a show against the best players in the world of which a veteran circuit rider would have been proud. The following year Sam made it clear he was not a flash in the pan. In 1938 he won eight tournaments, had six seconds and three thirds, and was the leading money winner on the year with over $19,000. Some of his contemporaries who did not have much vision for either Sam or the development of the tour said no one would ever again win that much money in a single year.

Sam's victory in the 1937 Oakland Open, at the Claremont Country Club, was a benchmark in his career, not only for being his first on the game's competitive main stem. Along with his amazingly powerful game, he had a fresh look and manner that the newspapermen were instantly drawn to. Here was somebody different to write about, and have some fun with. A hillbilly. He used backwoods jargon with a twang everyone found refreshing. In Virginia you live in a hoowse, like to gander at peert young girls, and reckon Chalstin is the biggest city you ever seed before now. When Sam got wind of how the newspaper guys perceived him, he decided he would play it to the hilt. He was not alone in that gambit.

The touring pros of the 1920s and '30s were a unique breed of professional athlete. In no other sport were there players who, at their own expense and with no guarantee of income, traveled around the country competing at a game that was exasperatingly uncertain. However, while the purse money on offer did not in itself encourage thoughts of getting rich, for most of the pros playing the winter tour it amounted to a combination vacation and job fair. Almost all of them were professionals at private clubs in the Midwest and East. Their clubs closed down from November through March, and for five months those who were brave enough or thought they had enough game went out West and through the South playing tournaments. But it was also a chance to meet other pros and swap teaching ideas and techniques, and to find out about job openings that might be better than the ones they had. If they played well enough to get their names in the paper, that also opened up better club jobs. But they didn't depend on only that. They did whatever else they could to get a mention in the press. Like spreading a catchy nickname, or a reputation for being "colorful."

Ky Laffoon was a fine tour player of the era, but he also made himself out to be an American Indian, because he thought it would catch more press attention. He was right. He also had some physiognomy going for him—high, flattish cheekbones and rather Asiatic eyes. He also became very red when in the sun a lot. In Boston one year, a sportswriter noted Ky's appearance and his name, which sounded Indian, and asked him if he had "injun" blood. Ky, which was his middle name (his first name was George), said sure. In fact, his heritage was Walloon, a Celtic people from southern Belgium, but he let it be known that he was from an Oklahoma tribe. To further the image, he began to call everyone Chief. It all brought Ky a good bit of newspaper coverage, especially when he won or finished high in a tournament.

Sam Snead did something of the same kind. He played the hillbilly number on the circuit—although, in fact, he didn't have to try very hard. He was helped along hugely by Fred Corcoran, who had taken over as manager of the tour at the same time Sam came out. Corcoran was a feisty Irishman from Boston whom everyone took, or mistook, for a sportswriter. In fact, he got his start in golf as a scoreboard keeper with a knack for colorful lettering and numbering. But he was also a master promoter of and publicist for himself and whatever or whomever he was given to promote. He worked his way into the good graces of George Jacobus, a powerhouse president of the PGA of America, which administered the pro tour from 1935 through 1969. Jacobus hired Corcoran to manage the tour on the road—to search out tournament sponsors, make travel and housing arrangements for the pros, distribute the prize money, and get the press to write it up.

When Sam Snead emerged in Oakland, coming from off the pace to defeat Ralph Guldahl at the Claremont Country Club, he was immediately inundated with exhibition offers. They would be not only lucrative, but also sure money. Very enticing. Jacobus, recognizing in Snead someone whose presence in the tournament field every week would spark business at the gate, was not going to let that happen. To make sure Sam played in those tournaments he told Corcoran to propose himself to Sam as his personal manager. Sam liked Fred, and they shook hands on it. Corcoran would manage Sam, without a written contract, for some twenty years. He would also go on to manage Ted Williams and Babe Didrikson Zaharias, and help put the Ladies Professional Golf Association, the LPGA, together.

However, at the time the Snead-Corcoran connection involved a conflict of interest. Having the manager of the tour also managing one of the players hurt Sam's standing among the other tour pros. They bitched that Corcoran was seeing to it that Sam got the best starting times, had first crack at side-money exhibitions, was first choice for the few endorsement deals that came along. What these grudge-holders also realized but hated to admit was that Sam was "the show"; he drew crowds, and that helped their cause, too.

One of Corcoran's first deeds on behalf of Sam and the tour was to pick up on a comment Sam supposedly made the day after he won the Oakland Open. He was told his picture was in the *New York Times*, and Sam wondered aloud in the company of others how they could get his picture in that paper since he had never been in New York. A great line, quintessential hillbilly naïveté. Sam would say in later years that he knew about wire photos and all, that he wasn't all that naive, but he let the story go. In fact, the latest research shows that there was no picture of Sam in the *Times* in the issue in which his victory in Oakland was reported. Nor did his picture accompany the report of his victory the following week in the inaugural Bing Crosby Pro-Am. Perhaps someone told Sam his picture *might* get into the *New York Times*, or *ought* to be in it. However the remark came about, Corcoran never tired of relating it. It has become part of the Snead legend. It wasn't much of a haul from there to have Sam posing in cone-shaped straw hats and bib-tuck overalls bending low to line up a putt he was prepared to hit with a hoe or pitchfork. Pure corn, and the newspapers lapped it up.

The Hollywood crowd that met Sam when he played in Los Angeles and in the Bing Crosby tournament also took a liking to him. He had character, was funny, was a good story teller who spiced up his yarns with some raunch, country argot, exaggeration. And what wonderful form. Fred Astaire with a golf club. With power, yet. Terrific power. They talked Sam up, made him feel special. He didn't mind at all. He was off to a tremendous start, and he would keep running at top speed for four decades. During that time, the name Snead would become forever synonymous with the game of golf.

2

THE SWING

THE SOUND HEARD WHEN SAM SNEAD HIT AN IRON SHOT was like the door of a Rolls-Royce slamming shut. The contact with the ball and the turf—absolutely simultaneously—had a rich sound unmatched in his day, or perhaps any other. With a driver the sound was different; it had more of an explosive quality, the brisk but definite report of a rifle shot. What made these audible expressions all the more enthralling was the sublime elegance of physical form that produced it. It was a crescendo of power at once balletic and immensely muscular. If all this carrying-on about a golf swing and its results strikes one as the dreamy twaddle of a golf romantic, so be it. Athletics has an artistic aesthetic no less than the arts themselves, and in golf Sam Snead was the game's Michelangelo.

History has shown that the best of the best athletes very often have at least one extraordinary physical characteristic they bring to their game. Ted Williams had 10-20 vision, which was one big reason he was one of the greatest hitters in baseball history; he saw better than most people. So did Jimmy Connors, the tennis champion, a 10-20 hawk whose return of a simple serve got better the faster the opponent's delivery came across the net. Jack Nicklaus was bottom heavy; his thick thighs and legs inherited from his father gave him a solid foundation to make his high and powerful swing, and, perhaps more importantly, to stand dead still when putting. Sam Snead was also in the custom-made category—very much so; he was built to play golf.

It was often said Sam was double-jointed, and that this accounted for his extraordinary flexibility and degree of upper body turn on his backswing. But of course there is no such thing as a double joint, as Sam himself said. He described himself as being "loose-jointed." Johnny Bulla had a somewhat more precise analysis: "Sam had longer-than-normal tendons." No one ever measured Sam's tendons, but this was probably the case.

When Billy Farrell once asked Sam what made him so much better a golfer than anyone else, he said, "My rhythm." But Sam's ability to stretch and bend his arms and upper body to the extent he did was a key element in the tempo of his swing. In golf, speed kills. The best players are never in a rush to begin the swing, and they have the capacity to delay the start of the downswing, to gather themselves before bringing the clubhead to the ball. Sam had that capacity, although the pause was hardly discernible to the naked eye. It is hard to do for most golfers, if only because they are too anxious about their performance and want to get the swing over with as soon as possible. As a result, they don't finish their backswing, which in turn makes for a too-fast transition to their down-swing. The farther back you take the club, the less likely will you rush it down to the ball. Sam took the club back wonderfully far. Sam's Strauss-waltz tempo was a product of his innate physical facility—those long and elastic tendons. But there was also his (and his family's) inherent musicality, and his intrinsic bond with nature. Sam was a superlative hunter and fisherman, and part of that skill is to never be in a hurry. First-class sportsmen accept that you have to wait for your chance; they understand the value of patience.

For all the natural or inherited gifts he brought to it, Sam also worked at his swing tempo, his timing, and his rhythm. He would sometimes practice and even play golf in bare feet, because it helped him with his balance, which in turn produced a smoother tempo. He also made a point of playing practice rounds with golfers who had slow, rhythmic swings. When he played with Ben Hogan, Sam watched him get set to swing, then looked away. Hogan had a fast swing tempo, and Sam didn't want to let that feed into his own action. There were other physical characteristics that aided Sam's golf game. He had ambidexterity, which almost all great and even just very good athletes have to some degree. Ted Williams threw right-handed, batted left-handed. Mickey Mantle was the best switch hitter in baseball history. In golf, Johnny Miller plays right-handed, writes left-handed, as does Greg Norman. Sam was a right-hander in everything he did, but his father was a left-hander, and from him Sam inherited left-hand strength. It is an ideal attribute for a right-handed golfer, because a strong left hand is more capable of resisting the tremendous force put on it with the right hand when the club is about to strike the ball. There are no guarantees; the left hand will break down from time to time and cause the ball to be hooked into trouble. But in the long run, a strong left hand is a big help.

Sam also had the advantage of long arms—he had a thirty-five-inch sleeve, a bit longer than usual for someone just under six feet tall. This also helped him make his longer-than-usual backswing. Sam was living proof of a golf adage that says long swing, long career, short swing, short career. Sam is still the oldest golfer to win a tournament on the PGA Tour—the 1965 Greensboro Open, at age fifty-two and ten months. Even more impressive, twenty-seven years after he won his first Greensboro Open (1938), at twenty-six, he won his eighth. At the age of sixty-two he finished tied for third in the 1974 PGA Championship; at one under par he was only three strokes behind the winner, thirty-five-year-old Lee Trevino. Sam holds the record for the most wins for a pro over forty—seventeen. He is the oldest ever to have made the 36-hole cut in a tournament, at sixty-seven in the Westchester Classic. He shot his age, and under it, in competition, with rounds of 66 and 67 in the 1979 Quad Cities Open. It is not likely that anyone will ever play as well as Sam did for as long into his or her life.

But here again Sam didn't simply let nature be his guide. He carried small weights with him on the road well before Gary Player made that popular, and of course well before the fitness vans that now follow the pro tours. He regularly did push-ups and stretching exercises. In his prime years on the tour he never smoked and rarely drank alcohol—an occasional beer. Even in his eighties Sam astounded everyone with how far back he could take the club when he hit his drive off the first tee as an honorary starter at the Masters tournament. People smiled, applauded, and nodded a collective "Amazing!"

Another component of Sam's physique that helped him to his pantherine swing, as golf writer Charley Price once described it, was pointed out by Buddy Cook. Cook was close to Sam as his assistant professional and bookkeeper from 1957 to 1970, and played many rounds with him. Cook noted that Sam's left thumb was concave. There was a deep, inward-sloping valley from the fingertip to the drum; most thumbs are fairly straight, but Sam's was banana-shaped. Thus, when he put his left hand on the club, there was a natural cup into which the heavy pad beneath the thumb of his right hand fit perfectly. The pad was locked in; it was secure against movement during the swing. No wonder he felt so comfortable holding the club very lightly. He knew he was never going to lose it.

Yet another endowment Cook pointed out was that Sam's right leg was about a quarter inch shorter than his left leg. Most people have one leg a bit shorter than the other (just as one foot is bigger—or smaller—than its mate), but for a right-handed person it is usually the left leg. What did Sam's shorter right leg mean to his swing? The ideal position of the right shoulder when the player hits the ball is to be "underneath," as the saying goes. The right shoulder is automatically lower than the right at address (the position prior to beginning the swing), simply because the right hand is lower on the handle of the club. But a touch lower and pulled back is even better. The feeling is like that of a batter with his right shoulder pulled back while waiting for the pitch. The less extra movement in the golf swing the better, and Sam was made to sit back and under. He couldn't help but be cocked and ready to begin his swing with a simple turn of his hips, and nothing more.

Which gets to the essential characteristic of Sam Snead's magnificent golf swing. It was built around a pivot, which Jackie Burke Jr. said in 2004 is something "we never hear about anymore." It is perhaps the most simple and effective way to swing a club. For Sam it began with a kind of downbeat. Just as a conductor taps his baton on the rostrum before ordering the first notes, Sam's right knee kicked a bit to the left. That got him in motion, broke the stillness from which a golf swing starts. Then, he just turned his right hip behind him (as it were). Sam's coordination was such that you could not tell if it was the arms swinging back or the hip turn that put the club itself in motion. He called it a one-piece takeaway, and that's exactly what it looked like. The right leg braced to accept the pressure put on it by the hip turn, and the downswing was a kind of echo—the left hip turned in the same way. There was no shifting of weight to one side and then the other, at least not the way we see it with most golfers. It was as though his body was turning in a barrel, an image made popular by the noted British golf teacher Percy Boomer.

People not as physically well-endowed as Sam are compelled to move their bodies sideways to some extent to build power; this does help, but it makes for inconsistency. Sam's flexibility, lightness of foot (he once said, "You play this game on live feet"), and great strength allowed him to swing in a barrel without any loss of power. Indeed, it made him more powerful by concentrating the force he developed.

Sam added a wrinkle to his downswing that was unique to him. A few golfers copied it after Sam came out, but for the most part it was (and still is) exclusively Sam's move. As he started the club down after completing his backswing, he bent both knees so that his body dropped downward into a sitting or semi-sitting position. The famous Snead "sit." He always said this came naturally, that it was not something he worked out, which makes it yet another mark of his unusually superior athletic instincts. The sit pushes the body's weight downward into the legs and creates a rock-solid foundation from which to deliver a blow to a ball with a stick. It was important to Sam because he didn't have heavy legs; his were more the slim "pins" of a sprinter.

Sam had enormous power. To think of the distances he would have realized using today's metal-headed drivers and hard-covered balls boggles the mind. Consider that in a driving contest once, using the old balata-covered ball and a persimmon-headed driver, his average for the three balls he hit was 302 yards. What was all the more striking about Sam's length off the tee was his accuracy. "He was the straightest long hitter we had ever seen," said Jackie Burke.

Another part of Sam's power package was his alignment to the target at address. Here, too, he was instructed by his instincts. The line of his shoulders and hips was directed at the target itself, in what is known as a closed position. In this stance, when the clubhead is placed behind the ball, the clubface is aimed to the right of the actual target—quite a bit to the right. However, the clubface must be aimed at the target *when it strikes the ball.* To accomplish this, Sam thrust or pushed his right shoulder out toward the ball at the start of downswing, just enough so the clubhead was moving down the line of flight and the clubface was square or aimed at the target when it struck the ball. In effect, Sam pulled the ball, and as we know from baseball, whose swings are related to those of golf, pull hitters are the ones who hit the most home runs.

At the risk of getting too technical or instructional about the golf swing, which is not the purpose of this book, in golf terminology Sam "came over the top." That is a cursed move (and term) for average golfers, who are prone to it. The difference is that average golfers thrust the right shoulder too much outward and thus swing the club across the ball from outside to inside the target line. This is why they slice the ball, their shots curving sharply to the right and away from the target. All conventional golf instruction is designed to avoid this. Golfers are taught to set up so their shoulders, hips, and feet are aligned to the left of the target. This aligns the clubface so it is facing (is "square" to) the target. This is known as the "railroad" setup; the line of the feet, hips, and shoulders makes up one rail, the imaginary line through the clubface to the target is the other rail. Ideally, from this setup, if the club is swung back to the inside of the target line *and returns to the ball on the same path,* the flight of the ball will be either straight on target or have a right-to-left flight trajectory, the ball starting out to the right of the target and curving back toward it. This is a more desirable trajectory than the slice, if only because it provides more distance. The railroad setup doesn't prevent coming over the top too much, but it does help avoid it.

Almost all golfers, if they don't think about what they are doing or are not taught otherwise, will naturally address the ball in Sam's closed position. It engenders a sense of power, a feeling that there is something to hit against, as the saying goes, meaning the left side of the body. Indeed, a large percentage of the game's best players are closed at address, and come over the top to some extent. Hale Irwin, Craig Stadler, and Bruce Lietzke are examples among current players; Bobby Jones and Jimmy Demaret are among past greats who swung this way. No one teaches being closed at address and coming over the top, but it is the most natural way to swing the club. And the most effective way, *if you know what you're doing or have the natural instincts to not come over too much.* Sam, of course, had the natural instinct. But he also knew what he was doing.

There was a notion among followers of the game that Sam didn't know anything about the golf swing, his or any others. This notion was another reflection of the resentment (or jealousy) that was directed at Sam throughout his career. It was a way of saying he was just a dumb-luck hillbilly born with a gift. As part of that notion it was also believed Sam didn't work on his game, didn't practice, because he didn't have to. Sam took considerable exception to these ideas. "I've hit two million practice shots," he once said, "so I ought to know what I'm doing." And he did.

You don't win as many tournaments as Sam did in a state of blissful ignorance. In his heyday as a tournament player, from 1937 through the early 1960s, except for a time when he hurt his wrist hitting a shot and had to take six months off, the longest Sam ever went without hitting a golf ball was a week. One year, not a single one of the 365 days went by without his playing a round or hitting practice balls. He was what is called in the trade a "feel" player. But how to define feel? It might be described as having a sense of how to function physically to produce a certain result without giving much thought to the mechanics of the doing, or being able to articulate those mechanics if asked. The opposite would be someone who thinks "scientifically" about how he or she swings the club and, if asked, will describe or articulate it in clear-cut "scientific" terms. (Scientific is in quotes, because the view from here is that the golf swing is not as exact in any respect as the swing "scientists" would suggest.) There is a certain intellectual snobbery among the swing "scientists" when they call someone a feel player. Ben Hogan, famed for his mechanical approach to golf, once said of Sam that he didn't write much golf swing theory in his instruction books, or talk it, because "Sam Snead doesn't know a damn thing about hitting a golf ball. He just does it better than anyone else." A polite ending to an otherwise condescending viewpoint, and a wrong one.

Sam was a member of the *Golf Digest* magazine instruction panel beginning in 1963. Another member of that staff was Bobby Toski, a one-time tour player who has become a renowned golf teacher and was one of Sam's good friends. Toski remembers that Sam rarely missed a panel conference, in which a dozen or so golf pros would talk golf swing and how to teach it. A lot of that was (and is) the stuff that induces dozing off now and again, but according to Toski Sam was always alert and making contributions. "Sam would listen to Paul Runyan, Jim Flick, all these gurus going on in highfalutin' language about the takeaway, the angle of approach to impact, and so on," said Toski, "and Sam would just say, 'Fellows you're talking trigonometry when all it is is arithmetic.' One of the great things about Sam is he kept it simple. He never made anything about the swing complicated, the way so many do who teach the game."

Joe Phillips, for over sixty years the Wilson Sporting Goods golf tour representative in the field, and thereby a longtime friend of Sam, remembered a time when modern-day instruction guru Mac O'Grady was trying to help Seve Ballesteros with his deteriorating game. "They were at Emerald Dunes, in Florida, where Wilson had a test center," said Phillips. "I passed O'Grady's car and noticed in the front seat a Sam Snead instruction book opened to a certain page. O'Grady was teaching Sam's stuff. When I asked Mac about it, he said Sam had the best swing ever." And apparently, Mister Hogan, he (and his writer) conveyed it well enough on the written page.

Sam liked to say that thinking instead of acting is the number one golf disease, but in truth he didn't just *do* golf. He simply blocked out all thought in the moments before he began his swing. Jack Nicklaus, who would never be described as a "feel" player, did the same thing. When asked why he stood so long over a putt before beginning the stroke, Jack said he was getting his mind absolutely blank. He must have had a lot on his mind.

When Sam talked golf swing technique, which he did a lot, including the mental side, he did so with down-home metaphors rather than the language of physics, geometry, aerodynamics, or trigonometry; he was a Will Rogers, not a Wernher von Braun or Sigmund Freud. J.C. Snead remembers his uncle talking about how he controlled his emotions, his swing tempo and "stuff like that." It was well before sports psychologists had come into the game. "For example," J.C. recalled, "Sam said, 'You know how when the pressure is really getting on you and you're starting to get that choky feeling across your chest? Let me tell you something, pretend you're walking on thin ice. You want to be real light on the ground so you don't break through. When you stand heavy legged, you can't move.'"

There's a kind of poetry in that. It also comes from Sam's own way of being. Ernie Vossler was one of a number of people who spoke with awe of Sam's walk. "He had the best walk I ever saw," said Vossler. "It was different than anyone else's. He sort of glided, as though his feet never touched the ground. And he didn't tarry. I couldn't keep up with him."

That isn't idolatrous chatter. Vossler is an earthy Oklahoman not given to hero worship, although he loved being in Sam's company.

Bill Campbell has never forgotten a tip he got from Sam. "He said, if you're tacking a carpet to the floor you give it a short tap with a tack hammer. But if you have to sink a tenpenny nail with one blow, you give it a long smack with a big hammer. The trouble with your swing [Billy] is you have a big hammer in your hands and are using it like you're tacking a rug.

"Isn't that beautiful?" Campbell continued. "Sam had a great eye for the swing, and a way of putting things. That's why the other players liked him, because he was understandable. No high-tech language." With fellow pros, though, he would spike the language a bit with his well-known profanity and wit. As he did one day with Toski, who is no bigger than a jockey and was coming out of his shoes to keep up with the big hitters on the tour. "Sam said to me, when I hit a good tee shot, 'Mouse, you know both your feet were off the ground at impact. If you keep high-jumping like that it's going to catch up with you.' I said my ball was right there with his, and Sam said, 'Yeah, but if you keep high-jumping, somewhere along the way that ball is going to be out of bounds.' Two holes later I hit one o.b. He says, 'I'm telling you Mouse, you better find that left foot on the ground at impact. It was higher than an airplane on that one.' So I said, 'Sam if my body was as heavy as yours, I could keep my left foot down. But when my body has to rotate so fast, something's gotta give.' He said, 'Put some fucking rocks in your pocket.' Don't you love that!"

Sam would ask Bobby Cook to watch him practice and see where his left hand was at the top of his backswing. "He didn't want it cupped at the top, because that causes a hook. If it was flat you cut or sliced the ball. He wanted it straight."

He told his son, Jackie, "When you get out of synch you never make a swing change, you don't fool with positions, just concentrate on seeing the clubhead come back to the ball square. If you start thinking about stuff up at the top of your backswing you're done, because it happens too fast."

In a word, Sam knew his swing, knew the swing, like he knew his name; he knew how it worked, and what was wrong when it didn't. When I got to know Sam enough to kid with him, I would ask him if he came over the top. As suggested earlier, the phrase has a negative connotation, and I was kind of teasing him. He always responded, with a touch of irritated abruptness, "Just a little," then expanded and said he always kept his right elbow in close to his side to control the swing path and keep from going too much over the top. If you examine photos of his swing, you will see just that. The right elbow is in tight to his side, and the clubhead is swinging out toward the target when the ball is struck.

Sam was an excellent teacher, again contrary to general thinking, although he was best only with good players. Joanne Carner, the outstanding LPGA champion, would go to Sam for a fix and in five minutes she had it. One day on the practice tee at the Greenbrier Sam showed Lee Trevino how to get more height on his shots. He told him to just stay behind the ball a little longer. He changed Nick Faldo's grip and narrowed his stance at the Masters in the spring of 1990, and later that year Faldo won the British Open.

Sam had a profound knowledge of the game, the swing, the equipment. On his workbench in the basement of his home on the hill, he rounded the lead edges of his irons so they wouldn't dig as sharply into the ground. One year,

Wilson introduced a new ball and had Sam try it out to get his expert opinion. Sam found the balls "falling out of the sky," not getting high enough and coming down much too soon. He suggested to Wilson's engineers that there was too much paint in the dimples, which affected the aerodynamics. Less paint was used in the next batch, and the problem was solved.

Sam liked to say he learned to swing the club on his own, that he never took a lesson, not even a tip. Ben Hogan said the same thing, that he found his way to playing good golf by digging it out of the dirt. Which is to say, practice, practice, practice, and figuring it out on his own. The players of the Snead-Hogan era did do a lot of solo swing experimenting, if only because there wasn't the quantity of information that's available today in the form of books, magazines, videos, and some fine teachers with good eyes and the right language. But the idea that the Sneads and Hogans were entirely self-taught is ridiculous. Just as artists take from the masters who preceded them and make something newer, or somehow their own, athletes spin off from the technique of contemporaries and those who came before them. When Hogan was struggling mightily to control the flight of his shots, he watched others to glean some technique he could use to help his situation. He asked a lot of questions of people he thought knew something. And he got direct, hands-on instruction from Henry Picard that was the most effective help he ever got. Picard fixed Hogan's left-hand grip, and after that he was off to the races.

Sam, given his abundance of natural talent (far more than Hogan's), may have taken less technique from others, but he did get one hands-on lesson that was vital to his future and may well have set the stage for his magnificent career. That was something he never told the world, of course. The pros of Sam's era insisted on saying they did

it on their own, and were obviously not going to acknowledge any help from others. Pride would not allow that. Skee
Riegel told Sam's tale.

Riegel, a short, solidly built athlete, took up golf when
he was twenty-three and became a fine amateur, then a touring pro. (He won the 1947 U.S. Amateur, a Western Amateur,
and two Trans-Miss Amateurs; won every match in his one
Walker Cup appearance; was low amateur in the 1949 U.S.
Open; turned pro in 1950; and in 1951 finished second to
Ben Hogan in the Masters.) In 1939 he was playing a round
of golf on the Cascades course in Hot Springs with Sam and
the Homestead pro, Nelson Long. Skee asked Sam if he had
ever had a lesson, and Sam of course said no, never. Nelson
Long begged to differ, and told of the time back in 1935 when
Sam was having trouble getting his driver airborne. He had
resorted to using a 3-wood in order to get some height with
his tee ball. "Long said that on a hole on the back nine he had
Sam stop at the top of his backswing. He then pushed Sam's
arms and hands straight up and high over his right shoulder.
He told Sam that was where the club needed to be. Sam had
been swinging the club more around his body, on a flatter
plane, which he probably picked up from watching the older
pros and others of that era, who still swung in the English style
to keep the ball low and under the wind. Which they get so
much of over there. Long said Sam immediately started hitting these big, high drives with a driver. High and strong."
Sam was rather mum after Long told the tale.

Nelson Long gave Sam a backswing position that put him
on track to greatness. It had a wide arc, with the club much
higher over his body than anyone else lifted it in his day. Of
course, Sam had the flexibility to get it that high, whereas
others might not. In any case, it's the swing we now see in the
likes of Tiger Woods and many of his contemporaries. What
is so astonishing, and this goes to Sam's own talent and dedi-

cation (those two million practice shots), is that he put the club in that slot with incredible consistency for nearly sixty years. Snead had approximately the same degree of control over the flight of his golf shots as the driver of a car does over the direction and speed of his automobile. That is not an idle comparison, because there is quite a difference between the two operations. The golf component is of course far more complex, and prone to error. A car has a fixed steering wheel to turn the tires precisely, and an easily manipulated pedal to regulate the speed. To hit just one golf shot well with a full or even semi-full swing, let alone thirty or more in a round, all the golfer's nerve ends, hand-eye coordination, muscle control and memory, mental state, strength, flexibility, balance, and rhythm, among other physical and mental functions, must be absolutely spot-on, each coordinated with the others. But in all that, you're dealing with a highly unpredictable system, the human body. Blood and adrenaline flows vary from moment to moment; a twinge suddenly occurs in your back; a thought that has nothing at all to do with golf pops into your head and distracts you from your immediate purpose. All sorts of interferences with the work at hand are possible. That is what made Sam Snead such a fantastic golfer. He hit so many thousands of perfect and near-perfect shots.

Ironically, it was also why he would sometimes get angry over a shot that to ordinary folk was quite satisfactory. In the words of Bill Campbell, "Sam had a much higher standard of performance for himself than most people realized. He expected to do everything well. It's also why he had a short-putt problem. His percentage of successful long shots was so high that he had many birdie putts from eight and ten feet. But he missed his share of those putts, and thought the percentage of success should be the same with putts as with the long shots." Ah, but golf doesn't work that way. Sam's attitude was (and is) typical of the great shotmakers, who find putting not nearly as challenging (which, mechanically, it isn't) and think it should be easier than hitting a fine 2-iron shot.

Sam had astonishing control over the trajectory of his shots. He could hit them high, not quite as high, low, sort of low, with a three-foot curve from right to left, a six-foot curve from left to right, with backspin, a little backspin, no backspin. Whatever was needed. He was especially adept at shots inside one hundred yards, for which he always used a pitching wedge; he did not like using the sand wedge, as most pros do. His touch for these shots, so important to making a good score, was often overlooked in the assessments of his game because his power game was so impressive.

Sam could also vary the distance he hit a particular club. With a club designed (by the amount of loft on it) to go an average of 160 yards, say—a 5-iron in Sam's day—Sam could hit it 110 yards, 125 yards, 180 yards, and of course 160 yards. Such variations in distance are accomplished by altering the speed of the downswing. This requires an exquisite sense of physical motion and feel for the club. Sam was not the only one of his contemporaries who could do this. Others were adept at it, and it was integral to the gamesmanship that took place in his era, as we shall see. But herein lies a strange anomaly in Sam's game. He had trouble selecting a club for the distance he faced.

A favorite golf expression, and commendation in reaction to a shot played is: "It's pin-high." Which is to say, when one has played a shot to a green, the ball has traveled just the right distance and finished even with the flagstick, the target. This takes a good sense of distance, plus the ability to transfer that into club selection and into determining how much force to put into the shot. Golfers who are pin-high a lot get high marks as "players." And yet Snead, the archetypal "player," who could do anything he wanted with the flight of a golf ball, was never quite certain of what club to use for his shots. How odd! It's the equivalent of an English professor unable to differentiate between a noun and a verb. Was Sam's vision off? Did he have poor depth perception? Not in his prime. His eyes may not have tested 10-20, but he had excellent eyesight. And yet, "Sam would hawk the bag of a 12 handicapper to see what he was using," as Bob Goalby put it. This is like Beethoven asking Harry Connick what the next note should be.

The overall consensus is that Sam didn't have the confidence to pick the right club himself. This made him especially susceptible to suggestions from opponents, who in the heat of competition would try to mislead Sam into pulling the wrong club, and often succeed. Sam needed a caddie who had a knack for helping golfers choose the right club. Such caddies were hard to come by in Sam's day. "That was the only thing about Sam as a golfer that struck me as not typical [of a great player]," Bill Campbell concluded.

In almost every recounting of Sam's problem with distance, the anecdotes have him hitting the ball too far, farther than he needed to. Mike Souchak, who for years held the PGA Tour's 72-hole scoring record, remembered a time Sam was playing the first hole at the Tam O'Shanter Country Club, outside Chicago, in the All-American tournament. He must have played the hole a hundred times over the years, and yet he was uncertain of what club to hit to the green. "It wasn't that he was farther or closer than he'd ever been before," said Souchak. "Just a standard shot. He looked in my bag to see what I was hitting, which was an 8-iron, and he took a 6-iron and knocked the ball over the fence behind the green and out of bounds. He had two clubs too many."

Bob Rosburg recalled playing a match against Sam for the *All-Star Golf* television series. "We had to tell the announcer what we were going to hit so he had the information for his commentary, and on this par three I said a 3-iron.

I was really going to hit a 5-iron, but that was what we did in those days, say one thing then do another to fool or confuse your opponent. Sam was easy, I must say, because he was always looking in the other guy's bag. He had already taken out a 6-iron, but when he heard my club selection he changed to a 5-iron and ended up hitting a 3-iron, which went way over the green, way over."

Sam had one caddie who could put the right club in his hands, and whom he trusted implicitly. It was a fellow named Jim Stead, a black man from Greensboro who was a good player himself. It was probably because of Stead more than anything else that Sam won so often at Greensboro. With Sam's clubbing problem in mind, some of his friends, according to Bill Campbell, made an effort to get Stead to caddie for Sam in the 1950 U.S. Open, at the Merion Golf Club, in Philadelphia. Stead was sent up to Merion to caddie at the club at the beginning of the 1950 season so he could be considered a regular at the club, and eligible to take a bag in the Open. However, when the USGA discovered that Stead was going to be on Sam's bag, it was vetoed on the grounds that caddies were assigned by lottery, and no player could bring in his own man, so to speak.

Obviously, this was before the players could hire caddies as full-time employees, a policy that changed beginning in the 1960s. Until then the feeling was that because only the best players were earning enough money to afford the luxury of a personal caddie who knew his man's game and psychology from being with him week after week, it was unfair to the lesser financial lights. The restriction was meant to level the playing field so players of Sam's standing didn't have that added advantage. Stead might have made a difference in the 1950 U.S. Open, when Sam had his best single year ever, winning eleven tournaments, six of them prior to the national championship.

Sam undoubtedly picked more right clubs than wrong ones on his own. After all, he won more tournaments than any other male golfer in history. Still, it was weird for so enormously talented a golfer not to have a lot of confidence that he could pick the right club for his shots. One might even ask how he won as many tournaments as he did, given the problem. Goalby said, "It just shows how good he was."

No one can say for sure how many tournaments his clubbing problem cost Sam. There was one standout incident, though, as recalled by Bobby Toski. It was in the 1952 Jacksonville Open. "I'm paired with Sam and Doug Ford in the last round," Toski related. "They're fighting it out for the victory. With two holes to go, Sam is one stroke up. For the whole round Sam is coming over to look into our bags to see what we're hitting to the greens, and at seventeen Doug says, 'Let's do a number on him.' In other words, we're going to mess with his mind. I hit my second shot, with an 8-iron, and say to Doug for Sam to hear, 'Man, I really nailed that one. Eight-iron. Perfect.' Now Doug picks a club, hits his shot on the green, I ask him what he hit, for Sam to hear, and he says, for Sam to hear, 'I hit me a little nine-iron, soft.' So Sam goes to his bag, picks a club, hits his shot, and the ball never touches the green. I don't remember what he hit, but it was two clubs too many. He airmails the green, goes way long and into the hay. He makes a bogey and they end up in a tie. Doug wins the play-off."

That was the Jacksonville Open, a standard tour event. Could Sam's uncertainty about club selection have been amplified to a much greater degree when he played in the U.S. Open, the one event that so bugged him throughout his career? We know of no incident when overhitting a green was a direct cause of his losing an Open, but playing in such doubt could well have manifested itself in an overall poor performance.

Of course, we do know of one instance when he was short in the Open, and what it cost him. And so we speculate on the why of Sam's problem with club selection. In view of the fact that he always picked clubs that were too much for the distance, that he almost invariably erred on the long side, we go back to the 72nd hole at Spring Mill, in the 1939 U.S. Open, when on his second shot he came up short and finished in the fairway bunker. From there he went on to make his horrid eight. We ask the question, could it be that for the rest of his days there was buried deep in Sam's psyche the memory of that mistake, and the disaster it led to? Was he always telling himself that long was better, even when it wasn't? There's an interesting piece of golf history in the club selection business. Until the 1950s, golf courses didn't have the markers so common today signifying the distances from various points on the fairway to the greens. The first such markers were trees with white stripes painted on them to indicate that they were 150 yards from the greens. The idea arose to speed up play. Golfers, and especially the tour pros as the purse money began to get interesting, were stepping off yardages all the way to the greens. Some would go the whole 180 yards or whatever, and then slog back to their balls. From painted trees they went to a variety of yardage markers, such as sprinkler heads in the fairways marked with the yardage from that point to the front, middle, and rear of each green.

At around the time this system was developing, a ranking California amateur named Gene Andrews began to step off his own yardages from the tees to points in the fairway, and from points in the fairway to the front edge, the back edge, and the center of the green, and put that information down in a notebook he carried with him during his round. He had other specifics—the wind conditions that prevailed, the type of lie he played from, etc.—and he referred to the notes during the tournament to help him choose a club to play each shot. As far as anyone knows, Andrews was the first to do this kind of accounting. Dean Beman, when he was still an active competitor—he was an outstanding amateur (winner of two British Amateurs, winner of a few tournaments on the pro tour, then the highly successful commissioner of the PGA Tour)—picked up on Andrews' idea. He told his friend Jack Nicklaus about it, and Jack, a very methodical player, jumped all over it. Everyone began commenting that Nicklaus read himself around the course. Because of Nicklaus's status in the game, everyone else began making notebooks. Eventually, tour caddies began drawing up rather primitively illustrated yardage books—a schematic of each hole—with yardages from various points that they stepped off. In due time, publishing companies began to produce these books in color on high-grade paper and with smartly done diagrams of each hole, showing the yardages from thirty and forty different locations. Nowadays, every golf course in the land has these reference guides for sale in their golf shops for as much as ten dollars apiece; they have even become souvenir items at major tournaments. Most recently, they have gone high-high-tech. Laser beam sighting devices are now available, giving the distance to the pin down to the last inch. You can't use these devices on the course during a tournament round, because they are considered artificial aids to play. But the players and their caddies use them during practice rounds and mark the readings in their notebooks. Shouldn't these notebooks filled with illegally gained information be considered an artificial aid? We leave that question to the USGA.

Anyway, all golfers in Sam's day simply eyeballed the distance. Which brings up the question of why they didn't (we, actually, since I was one of those to whom it never occurred) think to step off the yardages and make notes of them? It seems such an obvious and simple thing to do to solve a problem all golfers have always had, some more than others. There are golf traditionalists who say the game should go back to that, should remove the "scientific" crutches that presumably make the game too easy and put back into the equation a more human element. If you don't have good eyesight, or are otherwise distance-sight challenged, you would have to work something out within yourself to compensate. That's not likely to happen.

Jackie Burke remembered playing a practice round with Sam at Augusta National at about the time Nicklaus was making the yardage book popular. "Sam had a notebook and started doing the same thing. I told him, 'Sam you've been playing here for twenty-five years, and now you're going to find out what the distances are?'"

The point of this anecdote is to say that Sam Snead would always try something new or different if he thought it would help him play better. He was not stuck in any traditional methodology. It was a symbol of his fierce competitive nature, something the folks in the gallery did not always see because of Sam's jaunty style, neat smile, and down-home quips. When golf gloves came in, in the late 1930s, Sam picked up on them where Hogan and others never did. But the most studied and controversial example of Sam's willingness to try anything to remain competitive was his switch to croquet-style putting. He straddled the ball and the line of his putt, with his entire body directly facing the target. He cut down the length of his putter a few inches for this purpose, but otherwise used a standard-issue Titleist Bulls Eye model. It was his answer to the yips, those mysterious nerve tics that tend to attack golfers, usually when they get older, and turn what was meant to be a smooth stroke into a convulsive herky-jerk.

Billy Farrell was there when Sam put his croquet putting style in play for the first time. It was in the middle of the second round of the 1966 PGA Championship, at the Firestone

Country Club, in Akron, Ohio, with Sam leading, mind you. Farrell recounted: "I'm playing with him and Don January, and on the 10th hole Sam missed the green and chipped up about two-and-a-half feet from the hole. Don and I putted out for pars, and Sam had his little putt left. He jerked at it and hit the ball twice. But it went in the hole. He picked the ball out of the hole and turned to me and Don and said, 'Hey, how many times did I hit it?' He hit it twice, and that gave him a five instead of a four. If he had missed with the double hit, and holed the next one, he'd have made a six.

"On the very next hole, it's Sam's turn to putt and this time he straddles the ball; he goes croquet style. We were amazed. We'd never seen him do that before. He stayed with it the rest of the round, and hit some beautiful putts. It looked like he was going to hole everything. Obviously he had been working on it, but this was the first time he put it in play. In the middle of the PGA Championship! He putted that way until they changed the rules and banned it." The ban went into effect in 1968.

Sam didn't invent croquet putting. He got the idea from a little-known pro named Bob Duden, who was the first to use it in big-league competition. In 1963, Duden croquet putted in the Bing Crosby National Pro-Am (now the AT&T Pebble Beach National Pro-Am), and led after three rounds. Duden not only putted that way, he designed a putter for the purpose; it had a 30-degree bend halfway up the shaft. A few others then adopted the method. They included Pete Bostwick, a ranking amateur in the New York metropolitan area, and Ward Foshay, president of the USGA, if you please. And also Dean Refram, a touring pro, who said it solved a vision problem. It does in that you don't have the distortion of looking rather sideways at the line of your putt when at address. You see what's in front of you with both eyes, the way you do when you drive a car, for example.

But it wasn't until Sam Snead went to croquet putting that the method was banned by the USGA. Why wait five years? As the ever realistic Bob Goalby said, "Because those other guys weren't winning tournaments." Actually, Sam never did win a tournament on the PGA Tour as a croquet putter. But he was a very famous player and was bound to give it a lot of attention, which he did, and apparently that's what got the powers-that-be to take action. And he did do some impressive winning using the method, as in the 1967 PGA Seniors Championship, when he employed the "squat-shot" style, as some described it—Jimmy Demaret quipped that he looked like he was basting a turkey—and won by nine strokes.

Sam putted croquet style in the 1967 Masters and did well enough on the terrifically swift and hilly greens of Augusta National to tie for tenth. Not bad for a fifty-five-year-old, especially when you consider that twenty-seven-year-old Jack Nicklaus missed the cut. But that's when the uprising against croquet-style putting began. Sometime during the week of that Masters, Bobby Jones, the grand icon of American golf and cofounder of Augusta National and the Masters tournament, sat with Sam in a golf cart and told him that the putting style he had adopted didn't *look like golf.* He also said it was in violation of the rules. Sam said it wasn't in violation, and he was right. Soon enough, though, Sam would be wrong. Repelled by Sam's croquet putting, Jones mentioned his feeling about it to Joe Dey, the powerful executive director of the United States Golf Association. Dey, as we shall discuss elsewhere, was not an admirer of Sam Snead—quite the contrary—and was only too happy to try and quash him any way he could. Dey took up St. Bobby's observation and set in motion the process of banning croquet putting. So it came to pass that in 1968 the method, and putters especially designed for the purpose, were banned. The overriding reason was that it was not *traditional,* a spurious raison d'être that might well have been actionable if a professional had wanted to take it to court. After all, it denied him the right to support himself, and it certainly wasn't endangering the community. Thirty years later someone probably would have sued.

In any case, to put a more explicit point on it, the USGA decreed that one could not straddle the line of play, that you had to play the ball from the side of it.

When croquet putting was banned, Pete Bostwick said, "Well, this means I'll have to go back to tennis [he had been a nationally ranked court tennis player]; I can't putt well any other way." Ward Foshay, of course, did not demur at all. He said he was revising his putting method and was reading a book on (traditional) putting by the British champion, Henry Cotton. When Sam was notified of the ban, he expressed some surprise, remarked how it benefited older golfers, and added, rather poignantly, "Wouldn't it be great if I won the U.S. Open putting this way?"

Given how long it took the USGA to consider the matter, and when Snead began doing it, one might deduce that Sam was being punished for being Sam Snead. In fact, according to Frank Hannigan, who served as executive director of the USGA in the 1970s, there was some concern in the halls of the association that banning it might look like an anti-Snead thing. In any case, Sam didn't entirely cave in to the ban. He just re-jiggered the croquet method. He moved the ball to his side—his right side—and still directly faced the target. He didn't straddle the line of putt or play, and therefore was within the rules. Sam called it the sidesaddle method.

The USGA didn't like this either, but couldn't ban it because it would mean rewriting the rule just written. And, especially in view of the fact that Sam was the only one to go sidesaddle, it would definitely have seemed as though the association was out to get Sam. Sam putted sidesaddle for the rest of his days, and it surely added seven or eight more years to his competitive career. He won three more PGA Seniors Championships, the last one, in 1973, by an incredible fifteen strokes over Julius Boros, a two-time U.S. Open champion and one of the best tour players the game has had. Sam, at sixty-one, was 20 under par on a course—PGA National, in Florida—that had been the site of the 1971 PGA Championship. A year later, in the PGA Championship itself, he sidesaddled his way to a tie for third, only three strokes behind the winner, Lee Trevino.

The big knock on Sam's game over the years was that he was a poor putter. Or, a poor short putter. Or, even more pointedly, a choker when it came to high-pressure short putts. It is true that he did miss a couple of short putts that would have made the difference in the U.S. Open, although one of them was, as we will see, under artificially strained circumstances. It is a measure of how great a player Snead was that less than a handful of these failures left the perception that he missed a lot of them, and that he didn't have the nerves of a finished champion. In fact, he was a superb putter from over thirty feet; he regularly ran the ball close to the hole and left simple tap-ins to finish out. And he definitely could make putts of length when he needed them. One time was in the 1950 Los Angeles Open, when he forced a tie with Ben Hogan by making two excellent birdie putts on the last two holes. He also holed out under great pressure to force a play-off for the 1947 U.S. Open, as we shall see.

In the end, though, it was Sam's swing that defined his talent and was the indelible mark of his career. It really was a work of art, a rare expression of both athleticism and dance—dancing in place, Nureyev without the leaps, and a wonder to watch.

3

THE ONE THAT GOT AWAY

SAMUEL JACKSON SNEAD PLAYED THE GAME OF GOLF WITH great relish. There was no part of it he didn't enjoy. Every time he gripped a club he felt a small, sensual thrill from the textured leather and the perfect fit in his large hands. He didn't know the science of it, but he understood that by holding the club too tightly he would lose flexibility, power, the "whereness" of the clubhead; that if he held it lightly as he would a woman it would be more pliable and amenable to his wishes. He delighted in the fluidity of the swing itself, in how his arms and body coordinated so well in the motion back and through. He often likened it to his bones and sinew being coated with oil. He had known the exhilaration of the halfback breaking through the clutch of struggling linemen into the open field and outrunning his opponents to the end zone. He knew the feathery lightness of release when with both hands he flipped the basketball, and how good it felt when it went into the basket without touching the rim. He had experienced the remarkable sensation of making solid contact with a fast-pitched baseball and sending it soaring over the fence. But the stir that surpassed them all came when he hit a golf ball: the way it took off so fast, like a bullet, hissing as it rushed through the air and going so high and far. And solely as the result of his own effort. He savored the solitary nature of golf, loved that he needed no one to throw a ball for him to hit, to pave his way to the open field. Golf was all his own doing, and in his own time. He grew up that way, more or less, and was comfortable with it.

Surely it was at this very moment for Sam alone to do what had to be done, to play the final hole of the 1939 National Open championship, and play it well enough to win the title. Probably. He wasn't sure, and there lay the problem. He led the tournament at the start of the day, after 36 holes of play, and after the morning's third round knew he was only a stroke behind his pal Johnny Bulla. But in the afternoon's fourth and final round he played well and sensed he had taken the lead. If only he knew for certain. If only he hadn't played the previous hole poorly. Now he wasn't sure if he should be aggressive on this last hole, or play it conservatively. He did know that the players in contention were all very good and were probably doing well, so he finally surmised he would need to take an aggressive line of attack. He would take advantage of the exceptional power with which he could propel the ball.

He wanted to get going, but the large crowd following the players just ahead were slow in getting out of the way. He hated having to wait to play, especially in a situation like this. But there was nothing he could do about it.

"Hey, Ed, these Philadelphia folks don't have much hurry up in 'em, do they," said Sam to Ed Dudley, his playing partner.

Ahh, Dudley doesn't care. Hardly said a word to me all day. Why'd they pair me with him anyway? He was nine shots behind me. I should be back there with Wood and Shute, or Smith. Or Booboo.

How could I have left that putt short back there? Don't feel tense. Why should I? I'm the best out here. Sammy Snead of Hot Springs, Virginia, who's gonna be the new National Open champion. Whooo!

Homer'll gimme a smile for sure. Pop, too? Mom? A grin, maybe. That'll be all right. . . . Uhhh. Underwear's sticking around my crotch. Gonna start wearing those boxing trunks kind. Yeah, but they don't show you off as good . . . There's a cute one. Hey, cut it out, Sammy. Got some business to get done with here.

Wonder how Shute and Wood are doing back there. Not many people with 'em. Everybody's watching me. They like the way I hit the driver. Lonnng. I'll give 'em one here 'cause I think I need to birdie this hole. Nelson's got all those folks with him just ahead holding me up, so he must be doing some good. They weren't with him at the start. Sheeeit, he's gonna do what Guldahl did to me in Detroit. Had it all wrapped up and that big bugger comes rolling in with 69. Then last April at the Masters, same deal. Guldy.

Well, like they say in baseball, you can't never have enough runs. Same with birdies. So I'll get one here and that should do it. I can get to this green in two. Gotta little breeze behind, fairway's got some run in it. If I tag one good here I'm home . . . Wonder if Homer knows how I'm doin'. And Pete and Jesse. And Janny. Oh Janny's gotta know. Maybe Homer put that radio up so everybody can hear how Sammy Snead is doing. They got it on the radio?

Okay, we can go now. Ed's up. Where'd that little filly go? Sam! Dogdam it. For later . . . Jeezus Dudley, hit the damn thing. You ever see such a methodical sonvabitch. Takes for goddamn ever. Dudley. Huh. Mom's maiden name. Hope she's okay. Worked so hard all her days. I'll win this thing and buy her a house.

Thwock!

Not a bad little drive by Mister Dudley. 'Course he's got no pressure on him . . . Okay, Sammy, here goes. Tee it up a little higher so I can spank the little bugger up in the air. Get me a birdie and won't that be good. Ummmmm . . . Gonna taaaake a sentimenntaal journeyyyyy, sentimentalll . . .

Thwock!

Gahhhh damn. Hooked it! Tried to hit it too hard . . . It'll be in the long grass. Yeah, but the people been walking over there, tromping the grass down. Damn, shouldna tried to hit it so hard.

The gallery, like a flock of birds on signal, rushed as if one toward Snead's ball. They swallowed up the golfer, but not for long. Sam Snead always walked fast, and now a little more so.

Why'd I try to hit it so hard? Wanted to get close, that's why. Ahh, somebody moved on my backswing. Saw it outta the corner of my eye. I don't hook like that when I need it . . . Yes I do. I'll make up for it here.

Jeezus, I'm shaking like a leaf. What the hell, I've been in tight spots before. . . . Damn underwear. . . . I'm too young to be gettin' bald. Is that why Pop never lets nobody touch his head? So he'll keep his hair? Hmmm. What they like in bed? Used to hear the squeaking once in awhile. Been awhile. Did I see that ball jump up when it hit in there? Aww, any kind of decent lie I'll get it up. I can hit it out of anything. Can't understand this shakin' though.

Gonnna taaake a. . . . Next one I'll get the rhythm. Sentimentallll juur ur ur neee home. Wrist is feelin' weak. Football. Coach Bell had it right. Go into golf. It's been good so far. Puttin' some money away. Audrey likes to dress up. So do I. Audrey. Fightin' all the time. C'mon folks, let me in there to see what I got.

The gallery made a horseshoe around the back of his ball, six deep and close in. He had just enough room to swing.

Well, let's see what I got here. Ball's down a little. Grass is kind of thin, not much cushion under it. Sand. Hmmm. Ahhh, old Sammy Snead can handle that. I got to get home. I'll hit the brassie. It's got that extra loft on it.

I guess it's my shot. Can't see Dudley for all these people. Nelson's puttin' out. Wonder how he finished. Maybe I should go with a five-iron. Put it up thirty, forty yards short and have a little pitch in. Nahhhh, I'm goin' for it. Hit down on it and run it right up onto that green. That's my game.

Thwock!

Hey . . . No. Ohh, shitdamn.

"GIDDYAP! GIDDYAP!"

Didn't catch enough of it. Thought I got it all. Bunker! Sheeit!

"C'mon, let me get through here. I got to get to my ball."

Just barely saw it finish with all of 'em crowdin' up in front of me. Bunkers stink. Sand's too soft. Ball gets down in it. . . . Fried egg? Maybe I got lucky. GOT to get the next one home. . . . Shouldna tried to hit that driver so hard. You know damn well you hit it further when you go slow. . . . Five-iron was the shot, not the brassie. Jeezdamn, now I'm really shakin'.

"C'mon. Let me through."

Oughta have some people keeping the crowd back.

Snead's ball finished at the far end of the bunker and was sitting down a bit in a slight crater. What's more, his ball was only a couple of yards from the front wall of the bunker, which rose some three feet higher than the point where his ball lay. He would have to make sure his ball rose high enough as soon as he hit it to clear the wall. There were murmurs in the gallery hunkered around the bunker. Sam could hear a few of their remarks.

"It'll take some doing to get over that lip if he wants to reach the green."

"Yeah, with his ball down a little."

"Well, he's a pro. He should be able to handle it. That's what they get paid for."

Yeah, right. Can I get the eight-iron up fast enough? Goin' a little uphill. That'll help. Except it takes up distance. Wedge'll clear it for sure, but it won't get me home. No, eight. I gotta chance it.

Choke down a little on the club. Ball back off the right foot. Smooth now.

Thwock!

*Ohhhhh, jeeezus . . . Ohhhhh momma, momma Sammy's not
doing good. Ohhhhhhh. Where'd it end up?*

Snead looked to see where his ball went. A person in the
gallery told him. "It's in the sod atop the bunker, son."

*Knew I shouldna hit the eight. Thinned it. Ball was down in
that crater. Sheeit. Now look at where the damn thing is. Chrissakes,
how do you get the thing out of that? Ohhhhh.*

Sam's ball was stuck between two slabs of sod that had
only recently been put in place. There had not been enough
time for the slabs to knit together and make a whole.

*Can I get to it? Yeah, but the hell knows where it'll go. What do
I lie? Three. Hack it out and hole the next one. Maybe a five'll be good
enough. Damn but I wish I knew where I stood. Ohhh momma.*

"Isn't he the fella Guldahl caught a couple of years ago in
the Open, up in Detroit? Think he's thinking about that?"

"I think he's thinking whether he can chop it out of that
sod. He should be able to, he's a strong young fella."

"Yeah, but it'll be hard to control where it goes. Seems
funny they should have it like that for the national championship. You'd think they'da done that work a couple of months
ago."

"Ahh, he shouldn't have been there in the first place."

"Yeah, I suppose."

*Sheeit, this is just hit and hope. No idea where it's goin'. Just
move it forward.*

*Get planted so I don't fall on my ass and miss it altogether. One
foot in, one foot out.*

Thwock!

*Geez look at that thing go. Got more on it than I expected. Yeah,
but its headin' right for that bunker. And goin' in. Ohhhhh brother,
what a way to finish. What a way to finish. Gaaa-damm! Momma,
momma, what's your Sammy done!*

Snead was not walking quickly now. As he left the bunker he lurched down the hill, then found his balance and

slouched on. His shoulders slumped forward, and he dragged his club on the ground behind him like a frozen leash. He kicked at the ground as he slunk toward his ball.

If I'da hit the driver easier. . . . sheeit . . . my game's to hit it hard. The lie in the bunker is what got me. Sand from some kid's sandbox. Or the beach. People here don't know how to condition a course and they're running the national championship. If that sod had knitted, my ball would have run down the hill into the rough and I'da had a chance from there. All these people crowding in on me so you can't think. What's Homer going to say? Mom'll ask me why I lost. Janny won't. Not Janny. Audrey. She's liable to sharpen the knife. Damn!

Hey, shit, it ain't over yet. Can't give up hope yet. Don't know the score. Wished I did. Dudley didn't say a word. Nobody else, either. Keep at it, Sammy. Aaaa shit I don't have a chance. Nelson's making birdies all over the place. Like Goooldy. Maybe not.

Snead's fourth shot finished just barely in the bunker. The ball was sitting along the edge, but this time atop the sand. Small favor. He would again have to play it from an awkward stance, his body on a severe tilt.

"This poor fella can't catch a break. From one hard spot to another. Wonder if he's thrown it away by now. Shame if he has."

I'll hole it, that's what I'll do. Run this sucker down for five. What a five. Take aim you stupid goddamn hillbilly. You know what my chances are? Slim and none, and lookin' like a chump.

Thwock!

That's gotta have some grip on it. Whoa, whoa. Christ, green's like a brick. Look where it finished. Ohhhhh, momma, momma.

As Snead walked through a gap formed by the gallery gathering around the green, a spectator said to him, "Hey, Snead, you need to make a six to tie Nelson. He's the leader in the clubhouse."

The words fell on Sam Snead like a safe dropped from the roof of the Homestead Hotel. He'd already used up five strokes. He would now need to hole the long putt for a six to get a tie. It was a forty-footer, at least. The odds on making it were as long as the putt itself. Sam Snead's head was whirling, many thoughts coursing through it and one that kept repeating, that he came up short with the brassie. Short. Shit. He could make the long putt. It was not unheard-of to make a putt of that length. He'd made some even longer. Except they were not for the National Open.

That hole looks like it's a mile away. And as small as a small bird's eye. Which way is it going to break? A little right to left? Left to right? Left to right and right to left, then left to right again. Christ, it can go six ways before it gets there. It ain't straight, though. None of 'em are. Just long. Ohhhh momma, what has your boy Sammy done to hisself? Made him look like a fool that's what. Like a damn fool. A damn fool . . .

All right. I can't not hit it. One thing for sure, I ain't gonna be short.

Snead gave the ball a firm rap. The ball rose a tad off the clubface after he hit it, took a couple of small bounces, then began to roll. It came close to the right edge of the hole, but slid past and stopped three feet beyond. And with that it was over. He had no chance now. His whole body sagged when the ball rolled beyond the target. It looked as though he could not get to his ball without stumbling. He was out of kilter, unbalanced, an unusual state of being for Sam Snead.

When he finally got to his ball, he went through the motions of lining up the short putt and taking a practice stroke. But it was robotic, without real purpose. There was no purpose. His eyes were as dead as his chances. He slapped at the short putt, the ball failing once again to fall. He had no reaction. So what! He tapped it in from a few inches, for an eight. Four more strokes than he had set out to score. Might as well be a million more. Same thing. There was a rumbling of voices among the gallery—sighs, tsks, throat clearing. The people Snead came closest to as he left the green did not, or could not, look at him. Not for long. A glimpse, at most. Snead himself saw no one, saw nothing. Gloom and doom, the depths of despond, utter shame. He had never known such failure. He had played his share of poor shots in the past, made misjudgments, but nothing like this.

He made his way back to the clubhouse through a milling crowd rushing past him in the opposite direction to see the last of the play. Someone bumped into Snead and, while hardly breaking stride, said to him over his shoulder, "Excuse me fella. Hey, you're headed in the wrong direction. Couple of guys still have a chance to win it. Shute and Wood. C'mon." His caddie was waiting for him at the door to the locker room. He was a sturdily built man in his late twenties, wearing a white shirt and light-colored pants. He was tired. It had been a long day, 36 holes, and of course in the end a very disappointing one. He thought he had the winner of the National Open, which would mean a good payday.

Sam Snead looked at his caddie and saw the disappointment in his face. He opened his wallet and separated two fifty-dollar bills in the center slot. He took one of them between his thumb and forefinger, hesitated for a moment, looked up at the caddie, and pulled the second fifty out and handed the two bills over. The caddie stared at the money for a moment. It was more than he expected. He looked Snead in the eyes, nodded his head, murmured a thank-you, and said in a low voice, "I'm sorry it didn't turn out better for you, sir."

"Yeah, well, I made a mistake. I made a big mistake."

"You'll do better next time. I never saw anyone hit a ball the way you do."

"Ummm. Well, we'll see."

Samuel Jackson Snead of Virginia took his golf bag from his caddie, put his hand under its long strap, and slung it over his right shoulder. He angled it so it rode diagonally across his back, the way he had learned to carry a bag when he became a caddie. As he walked slowly past the clubhouse porch, his eyes did not wander. He didn't want to see. Or be seen. But he was, by two members of the club, drinks in hand. One said to the other, "There goes that Snead fella. Made an eight on the last. Cost him the championship, don't you think?" "Yes," said the other, "That's going to be hard to live with. Wonder if we'll ever hear from him again."

Sam Snead heard the last remark. If he had to answer he wouldn't know what to say. Not at the moment.

4

THE OPEN

ONE OF THE MANY RATIONALIZATIONS SAM SNEAD MADE in respect to his never winning the U.S. Open was that it was just another tournament. As he put it: "Shoot, you're playing the same players you play against every week. So what's the big deal? It's like the guy said, He couldn't win the big one. Well, Jesus, what do you call all those others? What's big and what's small?"

The point is well taken, but the U.S. Open *is* a big deal, because people think so. It's a human construct, just like a lot of things on which we place a high value and use to measure success or failure. As they put it in the mid-South, the U.S. Open *signifies*. If it was called anything other than the U.S. Open, or the National Open, as it was referred to until the late 1950s, it wouldn't have the same meaning. If it was called, instead, the United States Golf Association Open, after the organization that stages it, it would be an *association's* tournament and not have the same impact on the minds of golfers or the fans. By the same token, the Western Open in the 1930s and '40s was, in substance, every bit as much of a major championship as the U.S. Open. But its title bespeaks only a region of the country, not the whole place. The Masters' aura, and its high position in golf's pantheon of championships, derives in no small part from its title: how do you top something called the *Masters*? The cofounder of the event, Cliff Roberts, understood that well. His partner, Bobby Jones, thought the name was a bit over the top and was satisfied with calling it the Augusta National Invitational. Roberts knew that wouldn't sing a leading role. What's in a name, right? Relative to the U.S. Open, which rings as unto bullion, the St. Paul Open, the Miami-Biltmore Invitational, the Rubber City Open, no matter that the same players are vying for these titles, thud as unto blivit.

While the psychological or symbolic importance of the U.S. Open is largely a matter of imagination, there are some things different about it that can be measured and actually seen as distinctive. This was especially true when Sam was a prime candidate to win the Open—from the late 1930s through 1960. In those days many tour events were played on public fee courses—munis such as Keller Park in St. Paul, Rancho Park in Los Angeles, and Memorial Park in Houston. These courses had a lot of play during the year—thousands of rounds, in which millions of divots were taken and not replaced; the greens were kept thick so they wouldn't be trampled to death by the weight of the thousands who played on them. As a result, they were slow-rolling. The grass was a mixture of strains, many of which just happened by in the wind and were not suited for golf as much as for the picnic area in a public park. Such courses did not have the funds to make conditions any better.

To a journalist covering golf in those days, or a spectator with no other comparative frame of reference than the muni he played every weekend, and for the players as well, at the first sight of a Baltusrol, Oakland Hills, or any other

Open venue the week of the championship you knew immediately that something special was going on. The fairways were amazingly narrow, their aisleway slimness accentuated by long, tangled grass bordering their full length. Bunkers as big as two-car garages proliferated. And although you couldn't tell the speed of the greens at a distant glance, when you saw how gently a ball was tapped and how far it traveled with such little impetus, you realized these were not ordinary circumstances. Quite a contrast between that and the "tracks," as they were somewhat derisively called, for the Anthracite or Gasparilla Opens.

What's more, the basic designs of the courses used for the U.S. Open were of a higher order. They were all at private clubs, and in many cases were the work of noted golf architects who angled fairways, situated and sized bunkers, and located and contoured greens with the highest level of creativity. Furthermore, these clubs had a membership that paid significantly to play under the best conditions—on fine grasses all of the same strain (mostly), the bad seeds that did invade being summarily dismissed with poisons or scissors. When the USGA got through setting up these courses and further "conditioning" them for the Open—greens firm and fast, the tees set as far back as possible, pins tucked in corners or a few feet in from the front edge—it was all the more a departure from the tour norm.

Which is to say, an Open course compelled the golfers of Snead's day to make adjustments in their way of playing. They had to be more judicious in the use of power and especially accurate off the tee so they could play their approaches from the fairways. Then they had a better chance of controlling the flight and spin of these shots to greens that, ideally, were much firmer than those they played on the regular tour. The players most certainly had to find a delicate touch with the putter. A significant downhill putt at Rancho Park didn't roll as fast as an uphiller at such perilous U.S. Open venues as Medinah Country Club or Oakmont Country Club. The abrupt pop-stroke for the heavier greens at the Greensboro Opens of the Snead-Nelson-Hogan and even the Palmer and early Nicklaus eras was dangerous. Then there was the perception that they had to deal with these conditions in the most prestigious championship in the game.

Advances in agronomy and maintenance equipment have narrowed the difference between the conditions and architectural distinctiveness of U.S. Open courses and those played on today's PGA Tour. Week in and week out, today's touring pros play on magnificently grassed courses that are powerful challenges to their shotmaking skills. The Tournament Players Championship (TPC) course at Sawgrass, Bay Hill, and Muirfield Village are among many others as stellar in every respect as any U.S. Open course of the past or present. Thus, the adjustment to an Open course players must make is not as extensive or necessary as it was in Snead's salad days. However, Sam seemed not to notice the difference. Or didn't want to. There lies a significant rub in his clouded U.S. Open history.

For a championship he craved to win all his life, and went to his grave sadly disappointed that he never did win, Sam had a rather cavalier approach to the U.S. Open. Byron Nelson had a cogent insight on this: "Sam thought he could show up the week of the Open and just play. He never prepared for it, didn't make the extra effort to think about what he needed on the particular course—to hit it straighter, higher, more cut shots—the way Hogan or I did, or anyone else."

When Ben Hogan made his fabled comeback eighteen months after his near-fatal auto accident to win the 1950 U.S. Open at the Merion Golf Club, he did not carry a 5-iron. This is perhaps the most-often-used iron in a set, the one giving a distance needed fairly regularly in a round. But Hogan told me that he left the 5-iron out of his bag that week because he determined after his practice rounds that he wouldn't need it. That's how carefully he parsed a golf course and formed his strategy for playing it. (It was also, of course, a measure of how confident he was of his ball striking.) He replaced the 5-iron with a 4-wood, with which he played some excellent crucial shots. Sam didn't do that sort of planning. As Jackie Burke Jr. said, "Sam didn't think he would never win the Open. He was so far superior to anyone else out there that it seemed unlikely he would even have to prepare for it."

Bob Rosburg expanded on that thought: "Sam wanted to win it his way. He wasn't going to change the way he played. He thought if he couldn't win the way he won all the others, then to hell with it." In a sense, then, Sam was a victim of, or was cursed by, his uncommon gift for golf.

As the years passed and Sam was no longer a serious contender for the U.S. Open title, he came to despise the subject of why he never won it. It was invariably brought up by interviewing journalists, and so became a constant and irritating reminder of this one gap in an otherwise singularly triumphant competitive career. Unable to avoid the question, he developed a few more rationalizations. He would say that when it came June, when the Open is always played, he was burned out from having played so much golf. Could be. Sam played an extensive tournament schedule. He didn't miss many, if only because that's how a tour pro in the 1940s and '50s made his living. In the pro game Jack Nicklaus joined in 1962, you could begin to parcel out your appearances to eighteen or nineteen a season and reserve some energy for the big championships, because the first-prize money for winning a tournament started to get up to a respectable, comfortable amount.

Then, too, Sam may have been suffering what Bill Campbell has called mountain melancholy, a kind of gloomy, end-of-the-world malaise to which back-mountain people are periodically subjected. And the melancholy just happened to hit Sam in June? That's also when the Disaster of '39 occurred, too, no? Furthermore, Campbell said of his friend, "Sam had a certain mindset that was pessimistic. If something bad can happen, it will. And so, bad breaks would have an undue effect on him."

Another of Sam's rationalizations may have first appeared in my book *Gettin' to the Dance Floor: An Oral History of American Golf*. He said that if he had shot a 69 in the last round of every U.S. Open in which he competed, he would have won nine of them. I let the figure stand, because it was the nature of that book to let the people in it have a free rein to tell it like it was, or like they thought it was. For this book I have gone back to check the numbers. Sam completed the full 72 holes in twenty-four U.S. Opens (he missed only one cut) and had eleven top-ten finishes including four seconds. If he had had a 69 in the last round of all of them he would have won five, and tied for two. Not bad, actually, except we are talking about one of the greatest golfers to ever play the game, who will forever and for all time be the best to never win the U.S. Open. Whereas the quintessential Open player of Sam's day, Ben Hogan, had an average last-round score of 71.95, and the equally great Open player, Jack Nicklaus, had an average of 71.71, Snead's was 73.83. That's a big difference.

In a few instances Sam's finishes may have been affected by the pairings he got, which brings up his relationship with the United States Golf Association, and more specifically the powerful executive secretary of the association in the years Sam was competitive in U.S. Open play, Joseph P. Dey Jr. We will get to that as we go through Sam's Open history, covering each tournament not hole-by-hole or shot-by-shot but in an overall review meant to shed perhaps a final light on a fascinating subject.

1937: Oakland Hills Country Club, Birmingham, Michigan. It looked very much like Sam would cap what was a tremendously successful rookie year on the pro tour with a victory in his very first U.S. Open. He started out with a fine 69 to share the first-round lead with Denny Shute. He followed with rounds of 73-70, and over the three rounds was either in second place or tied for first. With a final-round 71 it appeared he had it won. He was congratulated to that effect by Tommy Armour, even before the rest of the field was in: "You've won yourself the Open, laddie," said the Silver Scot. Not quite. Ralph Guldahl, riding a hot streak in which, between 1936 and 1939, he won two consecutive U.S. Opens (including this one), two Western Opens, and a Masters, rushed home in the late afternoon with a three-under-par 69 to beat Sam by two shots. A 69 in the final round would have won it for Sam. It was a disappointment, of course, but he was just starting his career, did not in any way falter down the stretch, and undoubtedly felt it was just a matter of time. Then again, as Bill Campbell said, Sam had a way of not taking bad luck or breaks very well. Perhaps that was demonstrated the following year.

1938: Cherry Hills Club, Denver, Colorado. Considering that he had such a fabulous season on the regular tour—winning eight tournaments and over $19,000—such poor play in the U.S. Open seems very strange. Sam scored 77-76-76-80. Needless to say, a 69 on the last 18 would have been worthless. However, his star ascended once again the following year, only to take the dive of all dives at the very end.

1939: Philadelphia Country Club (Spring Mill Course), West Conshohocken, Pennsylvania. Sam opened with a record-breaking 68, followed with a round of 71 to hold the lead. He shot a third-round 73 to fall into a three-way tie for second, and played solid golf for the first sixteen holes of the final round. Going to the 18th (72nd) he was leading the field. A par five on the last hole would have brought him the victory over Byron Nelson, Denny Shute, and Craig Wood. However, he didn't know that as he prepared to play the last hole of the championship.

Sam would come to attribute the disaster that befell him on the 72nd hole to his not having known what the other players were doing, and where he stood in relation to them. Indeed, there were no scoreboards around the course, as there routinely are now. He also suggested that the players who were in contention were too spread out over the course for him to get a sense of who was doing what. Therefore, after bogeying the 17th (71st) hole, he became convinced he needed a birdie on the final hole to win, or maybe tie. It was a par five reachable in two shots by players who could hit the ball as far as Sam. With that in mind, he overreached off the tee. Trying to get as much distance as possible, he hooked his drive into the rough on the left. The real mistake, though, was choosing to play a brassie from the sandy lie he had for his second shot. Although Sam's brassie (2-wood) had a degree or two more loft than standard, it was still a difficult club with which to hit a high shot, even from a decent lie. But Sam had always played a bold, strong game.

However, with his brassie he put the second shot in a fairway bunker about 110 yards from the green. Johnny Bulla said Sam actually hit the shot well, just not high enough, because it finished up close to the front wall of the bunker. Others remember that the ball only carried some 160 yards in the air and rolled into the sand. Sam would just say he "didn't get all of it." The problem from the bunker was that the ball was sitting slightly down on soft, loose sand. But, anxious to reach the green in three, where he could two-putt for a par five and surely be close to winning, he again chose a club that would get the distance needed but might not have enough loft to raise the ball over the front wall. He would have to catch the ball perfectly, but he didn't. Under the pressure that was mounting, and because of the nature of the lie, he caught the ball a little thin—in the middle of the ball. It banged into the top edge of the bunker wall and lodged between pieces of new sod that had been put in place too late to knit completely in time for the championship. From there he could do nothing but hack the ball out and get it as near to the green as possible. Which he did, hitting it into a greenside bunker. Alas, it was yet another bad situation—an awkward stance with one foot in the sand, the other out.

From here on things came to a sad and ruinous conclusion. When he finally reached the green, in five strokes, someone told him he needed a six to tie Nelson. Thank you, but he had a forty-foot putt to get that six. He gave the putt a pretty good try; the ball grazed the edge of the cup and ran two or three feet past. Now, completely demoralized and realizing he no longer had a chance to win, he missed the short one and finished with an eight. Had he scored a five he would have won by one stroke. A birdie four would have given him a two-stroke victory. It was a hole that left a stain on Sam's psyche for the rest of his life.

As for the tee-off times and pairings, all the close contenders except Johnny Bulla were playing within two starting times of each other. On the final day, when two rounds were played to conclude the tournament and the pairings weren't changed between the third and fourth rounds, this was how it stood, with the player's position and total score in the competition after 36 holes noted:

8:30 a.m.–12:30 p.m.: Horton Smith (2nd at 140) and Bud Ward (4th at 142)

8:40 a.m.–12:40 p.m.: Byron Nelson (7th at 145) and Olin
    Dutra (6th at 144)

8:50 a.m.–12:50 p.m.: Sam Snead (1st at 139) and Ed Dudley
    (9th at 148)

9:15 a.m.–1:15 p.m.: Craig Wood (3rd at 141) and Gene
    Sarazen (8th at 146)

9:35 a.m.–1:35 p.m.: Denny Shute (4th at 142) and Lawson
    Little (5th at 143)

Sam might have had an inkling of how the other contenders were doing from crowd noise, or from actually
seeing Nelson, who got hot on the final 18 (he shot a one-
under-par 68) and was playing just ahead of him. Maybe
in such a stressful situation that is too much to have asked
of him. More to the point, as Jim Finegan indicated in his
Centennial Tribute to Philadelphia Golf, Sam later claimed
with a touch of bitterness that Ed Dudley, with whom he
was paired, "and others around me knew exactly how things
stood, but not one of them spoke up."

Why was Dudley paired with Sam, anyway? He was
nine shots behind Sam at the beginning of the third round.
It was probably because Dudley was the home pro at the
Philadelphia Country Club, site of the championship, and was
favored with a marquee pairing. Dudley was also a rising star
in the golf establishment, not so much as a player although
he was a good one, but as a kind of company man. He was
the first head professional at Bobby Jones' stiffly run Augusta
National Golf Club, a job he held for thirty years. Later, he
served seven years as the president of the PGA of America. In
this position of power, Dudley fought the tour pros when they
began the process of breaking away from the association so
they could run the circuit themselves. It was a bitter, rancor-
ous fight the tour pros finally won in 1968.

I am going to suggest a bit of a conspiracy theory in regard to Sam's pairing at Philadelphia in 1939, which was compounded in all future U.S. Opens where he had a chance to win. You can take it or leave it. In 1939, Joe Dey Jr. had been the executive director of the USGA for five years. He had by now carved out a powerful position for himself. Dey did not like Sam Snead, for reasons we will get into in depth later. Did Dey put Sam with Dudley because he knew Dudley would not be helpful in such areas as telling him where he stood in the tournament?

There was precedent for this sort of thing—or its opposite. In the 1936 U.S. Open, a dark horse, Tony Manero, was in contention, challenging the tour's most consistent player, Harry Cooper. In the final round, Manero was paired with Gene Sarazen, who as everyone recognized was doing all he could to help a fellow Italian win the national championship. Throughout the round Sarazen was giving Manero pep talks, and may well have advised him on club selection. Cooper, who finished second, thought so, but he wasn't the only one who did. Manero shot a final-round 67 to come from four strokes behind and defeat Cooper by two shots. Was the Snead-Dudley pairing conceived in an effort to avoid such collusion? Sam could well have been paired with his best buddy, Johnny Bulla, for the last two rounds at Spring Mill; Bulla was only four shots behind Sam after 36 holes.

For now I will say only that Sam should have been paired, if not with Bulla, then with Horton Smith, Bud Ward, Craig Wood, Denny Shute, or Lawson Little—in other words, with other players who were close to him in the standings. Dudley wasn't even close to Sam compared to the others. Except in the case of the Wood-Sarazen pairing, with its five-stroke differential, all the other pairings of contenders were of golfers no more than two strokes apart.

Obviously, a 69 in the last round would have brought Sam a victory, by three shots.

1940: Canterbury Golf Club, Cleveland, Ohio. As depressed as he had been when he finished play in the last Open, Sam showed a true fighting spirit with a record-setting opening-round 67. He led the field by two, and followed with a 74 to share the lead with Lawson Little and Horton Smith after 36 holes. And once again, the pairing issue was significant. For the last two rounds Sam was off last, which as we shall see was almost always the case when he was in contention. He was paired with Henry Picard, who was five strokes behind him, and Jack Ryan, who was nine shots off the lead. In any case, as if the ghouls of Philadelphia were shrieking in his ears, in the third round he shot a 73 to stay tied with Little, and then sank to a horrendous 81, the worst round, final or otherwise, in his Open career. With a 69 he would have won by four strokes.

There was little press coverage of Sam's 81, other than to say he more or less repeated his dismal final-round performance of the year before. His finish was overshadowed by the more dramatic story of Ed "Porky" Oliver, who tied for the championship but was disqualified because he hit his drive to start the final round before he was scheduled to do so.

1941: Colonial Country Club, Fort Worth, Texas. Sam was tied for second after 36 holes, on rounds of 76-70. But this time it was the third round that got him. He had a 77, and with a last-round 73 ended up tied for thirteenth. A final-round 69 would not have helped.

From 1942 through 1945 the U.S. Open was not played, owing to World War II. The PGA Championship was played in 1942, and Sam won it—his first major title. He had been called up to serve in the military beginning the week of the PGA Championship, but he asked for and was given an induction delay so he could play. The tournament was

Sam's parents: Harry Snead, left, and Laura Dudley Snead, right. *Sam Snead Archives*

Sam in high school, age fifteen. *Sam Snead Archives*

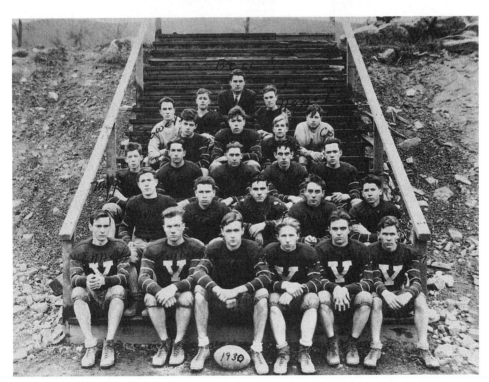

Valley High's 1930 football team. Sam is second from the right in bottom row. Coach Bell, at top, was very influential in steering Sam toward a career in golf. *Sam Snead Archives*

Sam (left), with Johnny Farrell (center) and Billy Burke on the first fairway; beginning the final round of the 1935 Cascades Open. Sam's expression reflects his mood after realizing that the owner of the Homestead and his head professional, Freddie Gleims, tried to distract him from his game so he would not win the tournament (and succeeded); he was leading going into this round. Burke won, Sam finished third. *Sam Snead Archives*

Sam accepting the winner's check and a medal from famed golf architect Donald Ross, for his victory in the 1941 North & South Open, at the Pinehurst Country Club in North Carolina. Far left is Audrey Snead. To the right of Ross are runner-up Clayton Heafner and his wife. *Sam Snead Archives*

Sam's pivot, a simple turn of his right side with no lateral movement. The gathered force his body position reflects is palpable. The club is high over his right shoulder, and a bit past parallel here with the driver. The overall look of this swing speaks of power with remarkable grace. *Sam Snead Archives*

At the 1940 North & South Open, which Sam won. He was always in perfect balance at the finish of a swing, the quintessential finale of his marvelous "dance." Gene Sarazen, in knickers, grimly impressed, follows the flight of the ball. *Western Golf Association*

Sam putting sidesaddle, a method he went to after the croquet method he tried was banned. It was his answer to the "yippies," one of a number of words he had for the frayed nerves syndrome. The stroke put some good years onto his competitive career. He even made it look good. *Sam Snead Archives*

Sam looking over his third shot on the 18th hole of the final round in the 1939 National Open. His ball is quite close to the front lip of the bunker. Using an 8-iron that he did not catch fully, his ball hit into the lip just above the sand and lodged in the grooves of pads of recently placed sod. He is examining the lie, and he was able only to chop the ball out with his fourth stroke; it ended up in another bunker, beside the green. *Al Barkow Collection*

Ralph Guldahl inspects the U.S. Open trophy, won over Sam Snead with a closing 69 at the Oakland Hills Country Club in 1937. It was Sam's first U.S. Open, and it appeared he had it won until Guldahl made his rush in the gathering dusk. Sam would look longingly at that trophy for the rest of his life, never once holding it as his own. *Western Golf Association*

Sam being congratulated for winning the 1949 Masters, his first of three, by (left to right) Lloyd Mangrum, Bobby Jones, and Johnny Bulla. Mangrum and Bulla tied for second. In this tournament the green jacket was instituted as a symbol of victory in the tournament. *Sam Snead Archives*

Heavyweight champion Joe Louis and Sam during an exhibition for military personnel during World War II. *Sam Snead Archives*

Sam is either showing Ben Hogan how big the fish was that he caught, or how long the putt was that he made. They were the titans of the game in the 1940s and '50s. *Sam Snead Archives*

Sam does his famous high-kick number among a group of much younger tour pros. His nephew J.C. is on the right. *Sam Snead Archives*

Sam playing his trumpet at a party in California, with movie star Fred MacMurray on the saxophone. *Sam Snead Archives*

Terry Snead, right, in 2005 with Pansy Gibson, his caregiver, and Carl Chestnut. *Carl Chestnut*

Sam with his son Jack. *Sam Snead Archives*

Sam with his beloved Meister. *Sam Snead Archives*

held at the Seaview Country Club, outside Atlantic City, New Jersey. In the final match, Sam defeated Jim Turnesa. Sam caught some razzing from the gallery as a draft dodger, because Turnesa was already in uniform (Army), and Sam's situation vis-à-vis his induction was not generally known. Immediately after the victory he joined the Navy. Like most other star athletes he went into the Special Services, which included playing a lot of golf with military brass and putting on exhibitions for the servicemen.

1946: Canterbury Golf Club, Cleveland, Ohio. The Open was restored to the schedule, and returned to the 1940 site. Once again, Sam got off to a fine start with a 69 that tied him for first. But he went dull after that, with rounds of 75-74-74. A 69 would not have helped. Meanwhile, he won five times on the tour during the year.

1947: St. Louis Country Club, Clayton, Missouri. This was one of the most controversial of Sam's Opens, because he was effectively gamed out of it by a clever Lew Worsham. It was played at a fairly short course by Open standards, at 6,532 yards. Sam played like a champion until the very end, when he missed a putt of 30.5 inches. He often got off to fast starts, but in St. Louis that was not the case. He had a first-round one-over-par 72, while such middle-range players as Henry Ransom, Melvin "Chick" Harbert, Harry Todd, Leland Gibson, and Otto Greiner had 67s and 69s. Among the bigger names, Ben Hogan had a 69, and Arthur D'Arcy "Bobby" Locke, the South African who was burning up the American tournament circuit in his first visit (he won six times on the tour), opened with a 68. It looked as though a new Open scoring record was in the works.

It didn't happen. Hogan scored a second-round 75 and never got back into it. Locke followed his fine opening round with a 74, and finished in a tie for third. Meanwhile, Sam steadied on with three straight 70s and was continuing his smooth golf into the final hole of the fourth round, where he found he needed a fifteen-foot putt for a birdie to tie Lew Worsham. Everyone remembered Sam's eight at Spring Mill, and the 81 at Canterbury, and there was the developing notion that the hillbilly was a choke artist who would never get over those final-round failures and make the most important clutch putts. Playing last, of course, he showed a lot more spunk than he was credited with. On the last green he rolled in the fifteen-footer that tied Worsham and forced an 18-hole play-off the next day.

Now things got interesting. For the first seventeen holes of the play-off Sam far out-played Worsham, who was scraping it out with amazing recovery shots from the trees and rough, and holing a lot of putts. They arrived at the 18th hole tied, after Sam missed a short putt on the 17th under suspect circumstances (as we shall see). Worsham's second shot to the par-four hole came up on the front fringe. Sam hit the green and had a putt for a birdie of the same length as the one he had holed the day before to force the play-off. Worsham chipped up to 29.5 inches below the cup. Sam's first putt was short, leaving him a 30.5-inch putt. The precise distance of each remaining putt is noted, because these distances were factors in what happened next.

After Sam's first putt stopped rolling, he moved into position to play the next one. He *knew* he was away, farther from the hole than Worsham, and had the honor. But just as he was about to stroke his short putt, Worsham stopped him and said, "Wait a minute, Sam, let's see who's away." Sam backed off. Isaac "Ike" Grainger was the USGA official on the scene. A onetime president of the association, and one of the most astute rules mavens in American golf, he related what transpired in an interview that I conducted with him in 1988 for *Golf Illustrated* magazine:

"It was a most unfortunate thing . . . They appeared to be about the same distance, a couple of feet. I'm lying peacefully on the grass just off the putting ring feeling sure we'd have another play-off, when I was rudely awakened by the confrontation between Worsham and Snead as to who was away and had the privilege of playing first. As an official, I had to say we would measure the distances to decide the issue. As to the story told by some that we couldn't find a tape measure and it took a long time to find one, I don't think that would be an appropriate view of the matter. Eddie Miller, of the USGA staff, was right there with the measuring device. But I do remember the conversation with Sam. He said that he wanted to putt first anyhow, and I said he couldn't unless he was away. I think what disturbed Sam was the initial confrontation with Lew. But what most disturbed him was when it turned out he was indeed away. That had a great effect on Sam's play. He missed the putt, and Lew made his to win the championship. On the other hand, Sam was putting from above the cup at 30.5 inches, which on a fast green with any roll at all is not an easy putt. Lew was putting uphill from 29.5 inches and could bang it right in.

"Whether Sam was over the ball or not [when Worsham stopped him] I don't know. But at least Lew saw Sam getting ready to putt and he took advantage of a privilege he had. I was not asked to make the measurement, but injected myself into it after noting the confrontation between the players. If Sam had putted first, under the rules of stroke competition there would have been no penalty, because there would have been no way to confirm the distances."

The overall time consumed before play resumed was about five minutes. A long time, under the circumstances. In a news photo of the episode Sam appears, at a glance, to be waiting patiently while the measurement is being made, leaning on his putter with his legs crossed and a hand on his hip. But a closer look at his body language reflects a very tense and upset person. As well he should have been. He was being jobbed, gamed, or in language Sam would appreciate, screwed, blued, tattooed, and chased by the Indians.

In today's sports lingo, Worsham froze Sam, made him wait before playing the crucial short putt, which gave him time to think about it too much. It worked. In the state of mind Worsham put him in, it's a wonder Sam hit the ball at all.

So, did Sam "blow" another U.S. Open? Was he the poor short putter and choker under pressure that many spoke of then and would call him forever after? Sam was not one of the better putters from the three- and four-foot range, but in St. Louis he was the victim of a rather egregious, but one must say cool, nervy piece of gamesmanship by Worsham.

Worsham was a good, solid tour player; a little above average but not anywhere near the Nelson/Hogan/Snead class. He was known as "the Chin" for the obvious reason; he had a big one that dominated his physiognomy, and also gave his smile a kind of slyly ironic twist that in fact mirrored a facet of his personality. Lew was a clever fellow, with a subtle sense of humor. In response to criticism in the wake of his action on the 18th hole in St. Louis, he said that the events on the green "have been described by some as a breach of etiquette, by others as gamesmanship on my part. All I can say is I have many fond memories of St. Louis, in 1947."

"Ike" Grainger also recalled that although Sam was naturally very upset about what happened, "at the prize ceremony he was as fine a gentleman as you could imagine." Indeed, a press photo shows Worsham and his wife, who is holding the trophy, and Sam with a smile and shaking hands with Worsham. Sam would say in the years that followed that he forgave Lew, who was just doing what everybody did out there in those days, including Sam. True enough.

Professional tournament golf in the 1930s up into the 1950s was a hardscrabble business. As noted earlier, in the 1930s and up through the early 1950s most tournaments on the tour paid between sixteen and twenty-four finishers, although the last-place player might argue the point. In the 1951 Miami Open, there was a seven-way tie for the last money place. This meant that $259.99 had to be split seven ways. It didn't come out quite even. Six players got $37.14; Jimmy Demaret was luckier, for he took in $37.15. Sam, by the way, won that tournament and the $1,000 first prize.

In any case, Worsham was like all the other pros of his day. He was introduced to golf as a caddie, developed a game, turned pro, and held club jobs in the days of the Great Depression. Money was tight, and golf was an especially tough buck. All of which inspired the players, if we can say inspired, to look for an edge in competition, some way to get the drop on the others fighting for the few dollars on the line. If first or second place was in sight, the gamesmanship got particularly heavy. (Worsham got $2,000 for winning the 1947 Open, Sam $1,500, and there would be an endorsement or two for the winner and a bonus from his equipment company.) For example, just when your opponent is about to draw his putter back you suddenly have this uncontrollable urge to jingle the coins in your pocket. Or, you wear white golf shoes and stand just within the field of vision of the other guy and cross your feet when he's at the top of his backswing. One week, Lloyd Mangrum and E.J. "Dutch" Harrison were pulling the walk-off caper on Sam. They would hit their drives, and while Sam was getting ready to hit his they started walking off the tee. Very disconcerting. After a few holes Sam told them, "Fellas, you better stand still 'til I hit or I just may catch one on the toe of the club." Which was to say, he was going to put a ball in one of their ears if they didn't wait on him like gentlemen.

In a book Sam did with Fran Pirozolla, he recalled that at the 1947 U.S. Open Worsham's gamesmanship began on the 17th hole, at least. Worsham stood very close to Sam as he was playing a short putt. Sam told him, "Lew, give me some air." Lew did, but Sam missed anyway.

Beneath his gentlemanly manner at the presentation ceremony Sam may have been peeved at Worsham, but he didn't act on it for very long. To someone with a more vengeful attitude toward a gamer, it might seem incredible that Sam and Lew remained good friends after the 1947 incident; they went hunting together for many years afterward. Sam liked Lew, maybe because he was a good hunter, a high priority in Sam's world. As for the gamesmanship thing, Sam would ultimately say, "*I* missed the putt."

1948: Riviera Country Club, Los Angeles, California. Jack Burke Jr. said Sam liked to get off fast in a round or a tournament, and sure enough, in four of his first seven Opens he led or was tied for the lead. He didn't quite do that at Riviera, opening with a 69 to Hogan's and Worsham's 67s, but with another 69 in round two he set a new U.S. Open 36-hole scoring record that thrust him into a one-shot lead over Hogan and Locke, a two-shot lead over Jim Turnesa, and a three-shot lead over Jimmy Demaret and Worsham.

In this instance, Sam's starting time was ahead of Hogan's, but behind Locke's. However, Hogan was paired with Lloyd Mangrum and George Fazio, two high-ranking tour pros who were four and five shots behind the lead. Locke was paired with Demaret, who was at the peak of his marvelous game and would shoot rounds of 68-69 to nearly catch Hogan and wily tournament pro Herman Barron, at 143.

Sam's playing partners were Chuck Congdon and Johnny Dawson. Congdon was only three behind Sam and was an excellent player who won the Western and Canadian Opens that year. Dawson was an amateur, and five off the lead. He was one of the best amateurs in the game, but the pros of Sam's era were never happy playing with an amateur, certainly not in such a big event. It didn't help that Dawson had rounds of 79-76 with Sam, hardly the kind of golf you want to be around when you're trying to win a U.S. Open.

In any case, either the pairings or the June malaise struck again. Sam went 73-72 to finish fifth, while Hogan went 68-69 to win his first U.S. Open. A final-round 69 would have brought Sam the title.

1949: Medinah Country Club, Medinah, Illinois. On an especially tough layout, Sam had one of those moments that once again fostered the idea that he was a choker in the Open. He didn't choke so much as make a questionable shot-selection decision. He played very solid golf through 70 holes and was tied for the lead as he played the par-three 17th. Cary Middlecoff had finished play, closing with a four-over-par 75 after rounds of 75-67-69, to hold the lead. Clayton Heafner finished a stroke behind Middlecoff. Only Sam, playing much later, had a chance. Two pars and he would gain a tie. On the 17th hole, his tee shot finished in the front fringe, just beyond the pond that came very close to the front of the green. He had a wiry lie in the fringe and was playing uphill, but he chose to use his putter. He came up well short of the hole, and then missed the next one to make a bogey four. He parred the last hole and tied with Heafner for runner-up, a shot behind Middlecoff.

The critics got on Sam for putting from the fringe, feeling he should have chipped with a heavier club to get more force behind the ball out of the thickish grass. Perhaps. In any case, a 69 would have brought him a tie.

1950: Merion Golf Club (East Course), Ardmore, Pennsylvania. This was the Open where it was arranged by some friends of Sam to have his Greensboro caddie, Jimmy Stead, on his bag. It was disallowed. Whether it made any difference is hard to say, although this was the best year Sam ever had on the tour itself; he won eleven tournaments, including the prestigious Los Angeles, Western, and North & South Opens. At Merion, though, Sam was never in it. With rounds of 73-75-72-74, he tied for twelfth, while Ben Hogan made his celebrated, hyperdramatic comeback to win the title in a play-off with George Fazio and Lloyd Mangrum.

1951: Oakland Hills Country Club, Birmingham, Michigan. Once again Sam took the first-round lead, with a one-over-par 71. This was the year Oakland Hills had been significantly revamped by Robert Trent Jones Sr. and made into what Ben Hogan, who won this championship, reputedly called a "monster." Indeed, Hogan shot a first-round 76. But Sam couldn't hold on. He went for a 78 in the second round, followed that with 72-75, and finished tied for fourth. A 69 to finish would not have helped. In fact, there were only two rounds in the 60s throughout the tournament, a 67 by Hogan and a 69 by Clayton Heafner, both in the last round.

With this championship another negative trend seemed to mark Sam's Open performances: he couldn't maintain his pace when he got off to a fast start.

1952: Northwood Country Club, Dallas, Texas. An opening-round 70 brought Sam a tie for third, but from there on it was all downhill. He shot 75-76-72 to finish in a tie for tenth, twelve strokes behind the winner, Julius Boros.

1953: Oakmont Country Club, Oakmont, Pennsylvania. As I've been suggesting throughout this recap of Sam's U.S. Open history, the pairings he received for the last two rounds were once again questionable. In fact, in almost every instance since 1939, when he was in deep contention he was sent off last among the other leaders. And he was not necessarily paired with those who were closest to the lead. A coincidence? In 1953 the trend (or conspiracy?) reached its nadir. This turned out to be the penultimate U.S. Open in which Sam had a realistic chance to win. It was also one where his pairings for the last two rounds were unfortunate not only for Sam, but also for the gallery attending the championship.

In the first round Sam shot a 72, which put him in a tie for fifth. Ben Hogan was the first-round leader with a 67. However, in the second round, Sam sculpted a fine 69 to Hogan's 72 and stood in second place, only two shots behind him. Although George Fazio was also at 141, no one else of note other than Lloyd Mangrum, at 143, was in contention. It was shaping up to be a classic U.S. Open in which the two reigning titans of the game, Hogan and Snead, would have their ultimate one-on-one for the biggest championship of them all.

But, either out of a total lack of feeling for the spirit of competition and sports dramaturgy, not to say the delight and convenience of the gallery whose attendance fees paid all the costs of the event, or to make sure Sam's chances were diminished, the USGA sent Ben Hogan out for the third and fourth rounds some two hours ahead of Sam. In the third round Sam picked up a stroke on Hogan with a 72, and when he arrived at the first tee to begin his fourth round, he saw Hogan going down the ninth fairway. Sam should have been paired with Hogan, or no more than a group behind or ahead of him. He had always suspected that the USGA didn't like him, in particular Joe Dey, and was not inclined to give him any favors. Now he once and for all felt sure that was the case.

Those still with us who were in official capacities with the USGA during that time—Bill Campbell, Frank Tatum, Frank Hannigan—acknowledge that the USGA was not very fond of Sam Snead. Better to say what they didn't, that it was Joe Dey who was less than sympathetic toward him. Bill Campbell suggested that while he didn't know what it might have been, something happened between Sam and Dey that created an enmity on Dey's part; Sam didn't hold grudges, or at least never announced them. He was in many ways a live-and-let-live person. Almost certainly, the something between them had to do with Sam's lifestyle: his profanity, and his sporting in public some of the women he dallied with, none of whom, as everyone knew, was his wife. Why should these things affect Dey's attitude toward Sam?

Joe Dey, with a very erect, chin-high posture, had not only the bearing but the mind-set of a minister of the church. It was a calling he had once thought seriously of following. Instead, in the early 1920s, he left the University of Pennsylvania before graduating to become a newspaper sportswriter. He was a second-line reporter for the Philadelphia *Evening Bulletin* covering golf when Bobby Jones won the 1930 U.S. Amateur Championship, at the Merion Golf Club, outside Philadelphia, and completed his storied Grand Slam—victories in the same year in the U.S. and British Open and Amateur championships. Four years later, Dey was hired as executive secretary of the USGA. There was just the right chemistry between Dey and the association, which was well known for its formal, patrician manner.

All the officers of the USGA were (and are) volunteers with professions to attend to, so the single-minded Dey was able to cement himself into the foundation of the association. With a very small staff working out of a cramped office in midtown Manhattan, Dey began building an empire for himself. He worked long hours, was an imperious taskmaster, and became a notorious chauvinist in his treatment of women secretaries. It would eventually be realized that he was a poor administrator, but by then he had become "Mister Golf, Ruler of the Fairways," as the *New York Times* headlined him in a 1955 profile. He was also pegged as a high priest of the rules of the game, although his interpretations were often considered improvisations, and he himself was never better than a 90 shooter. For the first thirty years or so of his reign (he left the association in 1968 to become the first commissioner of the PGA Tour), Dey oversaw all the details of the many competitions put on by the USGA. Among them was the pairing system, which was by all accounts of those who worked for him, more the result of whimsy than of practical organization.

"There never was a system, oh no, no," said Bob Sommers, a USGA staffer who worked for Dey for many years. "Putting the leaders together began after they stopped playing 36 holes on Saturday to conclude the championship [in 1965]. Prior to that, the leaders did not necessarily go last, either. Dey would start with the players in twentieth and nineteenth place, and worked down to first and second, then to twenty-first and twenty-second, twenty-third and twenty-fourth and so on up. The point of it? Don't ask. I never did see the logic of it, but that's the way he worked it. I can't imagine what he was thinking on that." As golf rose in popularity, the matter of crowd control at the Open became a problem, and the idea of sending off top players an hour or so apart, in the days before the gallery was controlled by roping (beginning in 1954), was meant for crowd control. But only for the first two rounds. Normally. As Sommers remembered, "There was always a suspicion that Joe didn't like Sam, and that he may have acted on that in making up the pairings. There was a clear sense, though, that in any U.S. Open in which he was a contender Sam Snead was not going to be allowed to put up a score ahead of any of the others. Especially Hogan, in 1953."

Dey, like everyone else, was well aware that Sam was on average not a strong finisher in the Open when he knew what he needed. Or so it seemed. The situation dated back to the 1939 catastrophe in Philadelphia, and Dey seemed to be acting on that in his pairings for Sam. As noted earlier, whenever Sam was close to or in the lead going into the last two rounds, he was last off among the leaders.

Does it sound sophomoric, the accusation or the idea that a grown man with such responsibilities would act out his personal distaste for a particular player? Frank "Sandy" Tatum, a former USGA president and for years one of the association's highly respected *eminences grises*, said, "I think it is quite possible that Joe Dey legislated however he could against Sam, because he didn't like him. I think Joe was capable of that. Joe was strait-laced, a stiff man of rectitude or moral principles."

We can add another element to the Snead-Dey relationship. Dey was born in Norfolk, Virginia, into a family that didn't have the money it once had, but retained the prestige of lineage. Dey was of the Virginia gentry, one of the more class-conscious segments of our democratic nation. Sam Snead was at the opposite end of that spectrum, a backwoodsman from up there in the deep, dark forested mountains of Virginia, where they had no education or respect for the genteel ways of society. Was there some class discrimination in Joe Dey's attitude, and in his ministrations vis-à-vis Samuel Jackson Snead? Could be.

Would it have made a difference if Sam had been paired for those last two rounds with Hogan in 1953? Well, in the three head-to-head matches they had during their career, Sam won all three, a fact of which he was always very proud. And, he won three PGA Championships when that event was played at match play. In other words, Sam was very good one on one, when what he needed to win was right in front of him.

Ben Hogan won the 1953 U.S. Open with a great final round of 67. Sam had an uninspired 76, to finish second. It was Sam's fourth runner-up finish in the Open. And yes, a 69 would have brought him home a winner. Hogan, it should be noted, then won the 1953 British Open, which along with his Masters victory that year produced the first-ever Triple Slam in American golf.

1954: Baltusrol Golf Club, Springfield, New Jersey. Although earlier in the year he had won his third Masters title, Sam was never in this Open championship. He had rounds of 72-73-72-73 to tie for eleventh.

1955: The Olympic Country Club, San Francisco, California. This is the Open in which the unknown Jack Fleck produced one of the biggest upsets in golf history, defeating none other than Hogan in a play-off. So astonishing was this result that it went pretty much unnoticed that Snead was in the running, and was in fact only one stroke behind the leader, Hogan, going into the final round. Sam began the championship with a terrible 79, but fought back with a fine 69 that put him four off the lead, held by Tommy Bolt. Sam then fired a fine 70 in round three to move into a tie for second with Julius Boros, a shot behind Hogan.

Bob Rosburg was paired with Sam on the last day, and at lunch between the third and fourth rounds he told Sam that this was one he could win. "Sam said, 'Nobody who has missed as many putts as I did will ever win an Open.' That I think was an expression of his fatalistic attitude toward the Open, and his winning it. Or inability to win it," Rosburg recalled.

Sam, who was playing behind Hogan (of course) in the third and fourth rounds and had complained about Hogan's slow play, shot a 74 in the last round to finish third. A 69 would have tied him with Fleck and Hogan. What a play-off that would have been.

1956: Oak Hill Country Club, Rochester, New York. It was as though Sam wasn't even in town this week. He had rounds of 75-71-77-73, for a 299 total and a tie for twenty-fourth.

1957: Inverness Club, Toledo, Ohio. Sam's third-round 69 brought him to within six shots of the lead, but on the whole it was not his week. He tied for eighth. A 69 in the last round would not have won it for him.

1958: Southern Hills Country Club, Tulsa, Oklahoma.
This is the one Open in which he missed the cut. He was now
forty-six years old, which for Sam was not all that old, but it
appeared his affair with the Open was on the wane. He would
give it one more good shot, the following year.

1959: Winged Foot Golf Club, Mamaroneck, New York.
The already very strong East Course was playing even tougher
because of heavy rains that softened the ground. Sam had
an advantage, even at his advancing age, because he could
carry his tee shots so far; he was not as dependent on the roll
after landing. And, too, the greens were more receptive to
approach shots, which were less likely to run off into the thick
fringes. Sam opened with a 73 to tie for fourth, followed with
a 72, then got himself into the thick of it with a brilliant three-
under-par 67 in the third round that brought him into a tie
for third. It shared the mark for lowest round of the tournament; only Bob Rosburg equaled it.

Again, Sam and Rosburg were paired for the last two
rounds, and here again Rosburg, who finished second, had
an interesting insight on Sam's psychology, attitude, and
point of view about golf and the Open. "Sam was four back
of [Billy] Casper after 54 holes, and off at 4:10 while Casper
was off at three o'clock. Hogan and Harmon, who were also
in it, were off at 2:07. The USGA was still not pairing the
leaders [and making sure that Sam was following them]. I
was also three back, with a chance. Sam caught Billy at the
turn and was even with him. So was I. Sam parred the 10th,
then at the 11th I holed from a bunker and Sam missed a
three-footer after that. Then on the 12th I holed a sixty-footer
and Sam missed from twelve feet, and it was over for Sam. I
could tell by his body language that he thought, here it goes
again, another guy coming out of nowhere with shit form to
beat me. Sam thought you had to have good form, and if you
didn't you were only lucky. The fact that I made those shots in

front of him, with my not-so-pretty swing, got to him. He liked swinging with style, and thought it was important in the final result."

Sam finished with a 75 to tie for eighth. A 69 would have gained him the victory by a stroke.

1960: Cherry Hills Country Club, Denver, Colorado. Sam was sounding more and more like he was destined not to win the Open, and yet the old dog would give it a good shot yet again. It was partly because he had a fierce competitive spirit, and was just so damn good even when he didn't have his heart in it anymore. The interesting, even fascinating thing is, after two rounds Sam was one shot ahead of the three new stars who would replace him and Hogan and Nelson as the game's next triumvirate—Arnold Palmer, Jack Nicklaus, who was still an amateur but on his way to the top, and Gary Player. Add a fourth, Billy Casper.

Alas, the June Swoon or Mountain Melancholy, or the 72nd at Spring Mill in 1939, got its hold on Sam. While he was still a stroke ahead of Arnie after 54 holes, Sam finished with a 75 to tie for nineteenth. Arnie, of course, shot his famous final-round 65 to come from seven shots off the lead to win his one and only U.S. Open.

Sam played the Open a few more times between 1961 and 1969, which was his last, but was in no way a factor. There was a wonderful irony, though, in his next-to-last appearance in the One That Got Away. In the 1968 Open at the Oak Hill Golf Club, at age fifty-six, Sam finished ninth (which might be a record for highest finish/oldest player) and in the final round, get this, shot a 68! Of course, it was his lowest-ever final round in the Open. It was as if to say that at this point in time all the memories of missed opportunities, bad choices, Joe Dey's pairings, and whatever else that stymied him in the championship, like an old soldier, had faded away, and he could just play without all the accumulated baggage.

5

CHARACTER

Sam Snead could be a very difficult man—ornery, curt, dismissive. He could be oddly cheap about something as inconsequential as a sleeve of golf balls, incredibly crude in certain social settings, and rather dishonest in making some golf bets. He was also extremely thoughtful of others, loquacious and funny, generous to a fault, and a scrupulously honest tournament professional. His attitude or disposition depended on the context of the moment—the significance of the event, how he felt about himself and the people around him, and his sense of how they felt about him. Sam lived most of the time in the present tense, and by instinct or intuition. He was like the animals he hunted and the fish he caught, and for which he had a remarkable affinity. His antennae reached out only as far as his immediate vicinity, to what he could see, feel, hear, and smell. He could sense danger, which in his case usually took the form of insincerity, of people looking to take advantage of him. Then he became defensive, abrupt, ornery. If his feelers told him you were nonthreatening, had a story to tell, weren't looking for a handout, had talent, respected his talent, you were welcome in his company. Then he told his stories, listened to yours if you had any, did business with a handshake. He was not always right in these judgments, but he was human, all too much so.

Whatever the circumstances of the moment, when you dealt with Sam Snead you didn't get any public-relations gloss. If he felt cranky, you got crank; if he was in a jolly mood, you got jolly. As Joan Campbell put it, "Sam was not interested in creating an image of someone he wasn't. He knew who he was and was satisfied with it; he wasn't going to be anybody else. Sam was Sam."

There were many sources of Sam's way of being. There was his nature, and nurture. Who can say how much of each? Sam's father, Harry, had a brusqueness about him. He communed a lot, in silence, with his Bible. But he would travel up to Waynesboro to visit his daughter Janet and his son Homer and buy ice cream cones and tell stories to his nephews and nieces. Sam's mother, while relatively more outgoing, had constraints. Laura Snead never traveled far from home. She was devoted to her duties as a mother, wife, and housekeeper. It was all she was interested in. A couple of times Sam tried to take her to Florida for a vacation, to see another part of the world. One time she got a little way down the road, but decided to turn back to her kitchen and her chores. She seldom left her hearth even to visit friends in town, although she was open to visits in her house by anyone at any time.

It was a close-knit family, and everyone rallied around any one of them who was in a fix. But the Snead household did not exude touch-and-feel warmth. Everyone was loved, but not in the show-and-tell way. They were of English heritage, after all. And mountain people. The physical environment of the Hot Springs area breeds a certain reserve among the people who live there. Even to this day, with a well-paved Highway 220 by which you can drive in less than half an hour to Covington, a small but relatively active city, the feel of Hot Springs and its surroundings is one of seclusion. Heavily forested mountain ranges appear at every turn of the head and speak of insularity and remoteness; the area is beautiful, but remote nonetheless. Hard winters of bitter cold and much snow add a claustrophobic element to life around the tiny community, even more so in Sam's youth, when radio was barely out of the womb and television was not yet conceived. It was then, and pretty much is now, a place where just getting by took all your time and energy and no little quiet cunning. When the prevailing society offers limited opportunities, you keep much of your life close to your vest. You don't tell anyone outside the family what you are up to, how much you have or are on the verge of having. What's more, when Sam came of age and went out into the larger world to make his way, there was a nice little Depression going on in the country—the world, actually— that further aggravated the straitened economic life of back-mountain Virginia. If not for the Homestead Hotel, even when business was down, the town might well have dried up and blown away.

Once he became a traveling man, though, and had come up in the world financially, Sam was always anxious to get back to where he came from. It was the only place where he felt really comfortable. "People talked about Sam's antisocial tendencies," mused Bill Campbell, "but you have to understand his natural habitat was rural areas, woods, friends who were not after him for this or that. When he went out on the pro tour he was fine for a couple of weeks, but the longer he was out there the more cantankerous and rude he'd get. I think it was his way of saying he had to get back home for awhile. I know that journalists who interviewed him in Hot Springs often said he was different there than out on the tour somewhere. He was warmer, more open, less guarded."

Sam once reminisced about feeling that as the sixth (and last) child of a woman who gave birth to him in her late forties he was a "mistake." It was more likely that his mother just had too much to do in a small, crowded household to pay her youngest a lot of attention. Sam's sister, Janet, gave Sam the motherly attention a young boy needs, and he was devoted to her the rest of his life. But his sister and brothers were busy growing up themselves, and as a preteen Sam was often left to his own devices. The feeling of aloneness was furthered by the scar above his lip that looked like a hare-lip, although it wasn't. He was born with it, and as with any youngster conscious of his appearance, it induced a touch of shyness. Preteen and teenage Sammy often went by himself to hunt and fish. This was his grounding as a man who would live all his life close to nature—his own and that of the woods and streams—even when sitting at table with the sophisticated and urbane.

He had friends in high school, the guys he played with on the football and basketball teams, and there was his girl-friend Audrey, whom he would marry. But in his culture it was the family that set the tone of life, and for Sam that included being by himself a lot of the time. People who spent any time with Sam in his salad days as a celebrated athlete came away with one overriding view of him, that he was someone who didn't need anyone, that he was content with himself. It was a way of being both inbred and nurtured, and served him well for the game by which he would make his living and fame. For those who want to play golf at the highest level, it is a game for loners. There are no teammates to coordinate with, or cover a mistake you have made. The ultimate responsibility for your every action is yours. A lonely business.

There was another element in Sam's singularity of man-ner that does not affect most mortals. He was an exceptional athlete, not just very good but uncommonly so. The possessor of this gift can only feel himself special, different from everyone else. Added to that was Sam's sheer physical strength and agility. Without trying, the body language and facial expression of someone absolutely certain of his physical powers says he is stronger, more efficient, better than ordinary folks. The latter often read arrogance into that carriage and are put off by it. Or, they stand in such awe of it that they maintain a distance between themselves and the superman. Either way, there is an inherent separation of states, with the celebrated performer on a pedestal, or simply apart.

Outsiders can relate to some extent to the physical side of such a person as a Sam Snead, even if they don't always know just how much actual effort it takes to reach his level. They can see the sweat of the effort on a warm day in July. The psychological dedication, and how that is manifested in the everyday conduct of such athletes, is not as readily understood. Those who elevate athletes to celebrity status do not realize that the wunderkinder themselves are vulnerable to self-doubt and are constantly questioning whether they can remain at the level they have attained. In the dark of night while trying to get to sleep, while shaving, having a meal alone, or even in the midst of a crowded party they ask themselves: Have I just been lucky? When will the streak end?

What appears to be supreme self-confidence to the onlooker is often a forced bravado intended to bury self-doubts. Whatever psychological track the athlete may be on at the moment, the mental commitment is total and exclusionary. To perform at such a high level is itself a selfish and egocentric act. What's more, the degree or intensity of concentration does not stop at the gate leading away from the golf course. It is brought home. Little room is left for others to intrude, including wives and children. A price is paid for such success in respect to ordinary domestic life, and Sam paid it, as did his wife and children.

In Sam Snead's era, the need to stay on top of the field
and the fear of falling from the summit were amplified by
the amount of money on offer. Modern-day golf stars make
so much money from one single victory that the pressure to
maintain the winning level is reduced; a break can be taken.
Not in Sam's day. Consider that for having won eighty-one
"official" PGA Tour events in his long career, not to mention
some forty "unofficial" ones, Sam's earnings total in prize
money does not equal the first prize check in even one tournament on the 2005 PGA Tour. Do all the fancy footwork you
want with the value of the dollar then and now, and it still
doesn't come close to evening out the disparity.

And so, when people in the gallery got close to Sam when
he was competing and he sensed that they wanted to ask him
about his swing, if he really hid his money in tomato cans, why
he never won the U.S. Open, if he could spare a ball, sign an
autograph, make a loan of a hundred bucks, Sam got irritable.
They were intruding on the concentration he needed to do
his business, to keep up the quality of his work. When journalists cornered him in the locker room minutes after his round,
be it a good one or a bad one, he hadn't had time to unwind
and could be short-tempered, impatient. He needed to catch
his breath. To his credit, while Sam did not suffer foolish
questions very well, and could put on an arctic expression of
utter disdain, he rarely if ever responded to the pests with an
insulting remark.

To some extent, Sam brought the pestiferous to his door.
Contrary to the ever-intimidating mien of Ben Hogan, which
to some extent was calculated to keep people away, Sam had
an engaging smile that appeared not infrequently when he
hit a good shot and the crowd roared; he wore his straw hat
at a slightly jaunty angle; he jiggled his eyes and had other
gestures of pleasure that were rarely seen among his contemporaries, who go down as one of the most grim collections of

public performing athletes in sports history. And, too, there was the image of the good old country boy that he himself promoted. In short, the perception was that he was easily approachable. Sam didn't quite understand that, however, and when the crowd got too close he glowered and walked faster. In the prime of his career people did better to enjoy Sam from a distance. Unless you got to know him. And that took some doing. He had to know where you were coming from, and what you wanted of him (preferably nothing). He had to feel he could trust you, and it didn't hurt if you openly recognized his talent. Sam didn't make casual friends.

Doug Ford recalled an episode that was indicative of an important aspect of Sam's character, and of how you made a friend of him or lost him. It revolves around money but has nothing to do with parsimony. Ford was playing a practice round with Sam at the 1968 Masters. Ralph Guldahl was playing in the group ahead, and Doug noticed that Sam was not and had not been at all friendly with Guldahl. It seemed odd to Ford, because he knew that Sam and Guldahl went back to the 1930s as playing partners in best-ball tournaments, and of course as rivals. Ford mentioned this to Sam, who then pulled a piece of paper out of his pocket that was folded in fourths. He unfolded it and showed it to Ford. "It was an IOU for $1,600 signed by Guldahl in 1939," said Ford. "1939! And this is 1968. I told Bob Goalby about it but he didn't believe it until he was on a fishing trip with Sam in Alaska and mentioned it to him. Sam whipped out that same piece of paper again, and showed it to Bob.

"The thing about it is, Guldahl never spoke to Sam about the loan. If he had said, Hey Sam, I'm still a little short but I'll get it to you when I can; or, let me pay you back ten a month, or anything that showed he remembered the debt, Sam would have told him not to worry about it, that he could pay it back when he had it. He might even tell him to forget about it. But when he didn't say a word, ever, that got to Sam. That upset him. It wasn't the only incident like that with guys on the tour that he lent money to." And when Sam did on occasion remind debtors of a loan, they'd get on a high horse and talk it around that Snead was a cheap sonofabitch.

People also got on Sam's case when they booked him for an exhibition that included a round of golf and a half-hour clinic, then expected him to stay over and have some drinks and chat. Sam didn't do the drinks and chat, because that wasn't what he was paid for, and when he didn't stay he was criticized, called selfish, ungrateful, a hard case. The Guldahl episode and the exhibition conflicts reflect a straightforward ethical standard by which Sam lived. You get what you pay for; no more, no less. Golf was his business.

HUSTLING

At the same time that Sam was hurt by those who did not do the right thing when it came to obligations, who were lacking integrity in their dealings with him, he had a reputation as a hustler who took advantage of amateur golfers when playing for money. There was, it must be said, something to it. More or less.

It is impossible to imagine Ben Hogan or Byron Nelson, Jack Nicklaus or Tiger Woods playing a pickup game with three amateur golfers whom they don't know at all and who shoot in the 80s and 90s. Sam Snead may be the only superstar golf professional ever to have done this. He did it a lot. The only proviso was, Sam had to have a money bet on the game. Over the many years, hundreds, maybe even thousands of amateur golfers from all over the world came to the Greenbrier, and to the Boca Raton resort, in Florida, when he was the professional there, looking for and getting a game with the famous Sam Snead.

When they got their date and were at the first tee the negotiations began. Sam did most of it. Make that all of it. The amateurs told Sam their handicaps, and Sam gave them strokes based on it. That put the game—the bet—hypothetically on a level playing field. It's a system peculiar to golf, and it allows players of differing abilities to compete. To make it as simple as possible for those who may not understand golf's handicap system, if one player has a 10-handicap, say, that means his average score for 18 holes is 10 over par. A golfer with a 4-handicap gives the 10-handicapper the difference between their handicaps—six strokes over the course of the 18 holes, each stroke falling on the holes rated on the scorecard as the six hardest. So, if the 10-handicapper scores a six on a hole where he gets a stroke, and the 4-handicapper scores a five on that hole, it's a tie. If the better player is a scratch, meaning on average he plays 18 holes in even par and his handicap is zero, he gives the other fellow his full handicap. Therefore, all things being equal, if the amateur shoots his 10-handicap score of 82 and the scratch golfer shoots a 73 or more, the amateur wins the bet.

The catch was that Sam made his bets based on the assumption that he was a scratch golfer when he actually had a plus-6 handicap; which means his average score for 18 holes was six under par—a 66 on a par-72 course. He should have given the 10-handicapper sixteen strokes, not ten. Needless to say, Sam rarely lost to the amateurs—his "pigeons," he called them—if only because the terms of the game were in his favor. Sam took in many, many thousands of dollars in cash— pigeon money—in these games.

How did he justify the fiddle? Or rationalize it? In good part, on the basis that many of the pigeons who flew into

Sam's coop were strangers from out of town who inflated their handicaps—sandbaggers, as they're called. In other words, someone whose true handicap back in California or Illinois is a 10 tells Sam on the first tee in West Virginia that he is a 15. That gets him more strokes from Sam than he deserves. Sam balanced it out by playing at scratch. Sam sometimes knew for a fact that these visitors were sandbagging him with a false handicap, because he would tell Buddy Cook or another assistant to call the fellow's club in California or Illinois or Ohio and ask after the handicap posted there. Very often, the fellow was a better golfer than he had let on to Sam. But there wasn't always time to make such phone calls, and Sam often relied on his good eye for talent. He could see from a fellow's grip or his waggle just how good he was. If the purported 10-handicapper molded his hands on the handle of his driver like a cashmere sweater on Marilyn Monroe, Sam flat out told the fellow he wasn't what he said he was and the adjustment was made immediately. Sometimes Sam would take the pigeon at his word, figuring even if he was two or three strokes better than he said, Sam still had a two- or three-stroke advantage based on his plus 6. So there was a bit of scamming on both sides of the fence.

Sam would sometimes make a different kind of bet as a way of catching out a sandbagger. Al Schwabbe, an old friend from the Greenbrier, related how it worked. "If a fellow getting up a bet with Sam said he didn't have a registered handicap, Sam would say that's fine and ask him how many pars he thought he'd make during the round. If the fellow said eight, Sam told him that meant he had a 10 handicap and he would get ten strokes. Now the guy is chomping at the bit, because he's probably a 5 handicap," said Schwabbe. "So Sam makes the bet, a twenty-five-dollar Nassau, say. The guy says fine. Then Sam hits him with a proviso. He says that for every par the fellow makes over eight, Sam is going to charge him fifty dollars. Of course, now the guy can't say a word. Sam did that one a lot, to get the sandbaggers."

Did the pigeons know Sam was better than a scratch player? Perhaps not. In the 1940s and '50s and even into the 1960s the handicap system was not as well understood as it has come to be. The average golfer simply figured a handicap was measured by how much over par you shot, and if you were a pro you didn't have one. Which is to say, you were a scratch. The plus handicap, which is a kind of oxymoron, was not that well known. In any case, the bets Sam made were not excessive. They usually ran to a hundred dollars, total, which was broken down into $25 increments, or "ways"—$25 for the first nine holes, $25 for the second nine, and $50 for the entire round. Four ways. It's called a Nassau, after the country club in New York where the system originated. There might be a press or two, an extra bet when there is little to no chance of winning the original bet, which would raise the total another $50, say, but on the whole it was not a lot of money on the line.

There was another rationale for Sam's so-called hustle. If someone wanted a playing lesson with him with no bet on the side, it cost a hundred dollars (Sam notoriously under-priced himself). Sam almost never did these, but that's what it would have cost. Therefore, Sam figured if the pigeon won just one of the ways, he was getting a chance to play golf with him for less than his playing lesson fee or to spend four hours on the course with Sam Snead for fifty dollars. A bargain if there ever was one. And if by some miracle the guy won all the bets from Sam, not only did he take money from one of the greatest golfers of all time, he had bragging rights among his buddies for the rest of his days. Even if he lost, he had those bragging rights.

Bill Campbell recalled a time when a Japanese group of twelve came to play at the Greenbrier. One foursome got to play with Sam, and of course lost. They paid with deep bows, and smiles on their faces. It was an honor to have given money to Mister Snead-*san*. The other Japanese in the group sought the same privilege, and offered him the same amount of money their mates had paid. They also wanted to tell their friends back home that they lost money to Sam Snead. "Sam would not take that money," said Campbell, "because he didn't earn it. Sam could do some wheeling and dealing in his bets, but he also had an honorable side to him."

The truth is, the pigeons didn't expect to beat Sam, and probably wouldn't even if the handicap business was legitimate on both sides. As Sam would say, if he kept it close for 13 or 14 holes "they're going to collapse like a sponge cake near the end." Which is to say, when the average golfer put his ball in play against Sam Snead, his pulse rate skyrocketed. Finally, Sam didn't feel especially guilty about taking the pigeons' money because the people who came to the Greenbrier and Boca Raton could easily afford the one or two hundred dollars he won from them. Which is another thing about Sam's hustling: he didn't play for big stakes, for "important" money, as the saying goes. And he never took the money of those he knew couldn't afford it.

At a Masters Champions dinner one year, Sam arrived and complained that his back was hurting so badly he couldn't make his usual entrance, kicking the top of the door frame with one foot. Bob Goalby was there. "Arnold Palmer pulled out two one hundred–dollar bills, threw them on the carpet, and said he was betting Sam could do it. Arnie asked if there were any takers. The bet was covered by a lot of people, including the shoeshine boy. So now the money is up," Goalby goes on, "and Sam goes over and kicks the doorway so easily that I knew he and Arnie had a little deal going. But the best part of the story is, Sam goes over to the shoeshine boy, gives him his money back, and tells him, 'Son, don't ever bet against a man at his own game.'"

In another incident with a similar ending, J.C. Snead remembered a game he was in with Sam and some other tour pros, including Roy Pace, who was not playing very well. It was during a practice round before a tournament, and in these games there was always some money on the line—twenty-five or fifty dollars might change hands. Of course, there was no handicap business in these matches. "Sam cut Roy up pretty good," as J.C. put it. "Near the end of the round Sam kind of eased over and asked me if this boy, meaning Pace, was making any money. I told him not very much, and Sam said to Roy when it came time to pay up, 'Oh, don't worry about it. I'll catch you up later.'"

Sam's percentage of wins in the betting games was very high in his favor, but he didn't win all the time. He always paid his losses, albeit usually on the quiet, in a dark corner of the locker room or some other dimly lit, underpopulated site. Pride, you know. On the other hand, Sam might do a little trick of the eye to make it look like he won. In a game at the Lower Cascades with Vice President Dan Quayle, a low-handicap golfer, Sam lost ten dollars. Sam handed Quayle a twenty-dollar bill. The Vice President said he didn't have change, but he'd get it in the pro shop. A few moments later Quayle came out of the pro shop and handed Sam a ten-dollar bill. A woman nearby saw the transaction and said, "Oh, Mr. Snead, you took money off the Vice President." And Sam said, "What's it look like." Heh heh.

His pride washed two ways. Vinny Giles, the Virginia native who was a high-ranking amateur and then became a player agent, remembered a time when his father-in-law and two of his friends played Sam. "They had a good day, and got Sam for about $200. Sam didn't have the cash with him, and they told him to just write a check. Sam said he wouldn't do that. He told them to wait right there, and he got in his car and drove over to the Homestead Hotel to cash a check, came back, and paid them off."

Sam never did like dealing with checks, especially when he discovered a few of those he wrote to cover lost bets were never cashed; the recipients framed them and hung them in prominent places in their homes or offices. Sam didn't lose the money, but he did lose his honor. Everybody coming by and seeing that Sam Snead lost to So-and-So or Charlie Whozzit was not something he cared to allow.

And then, of course, there was the matter of the Internal Revenue Service being able to trace checks, but not cash. Sam did hate paying taxes, and he always did, but he would try to improve his situation when he could. Not always successfully. One year an internal revenuer came to talk with Sam about his latest return. Sam figured he'd butter the fellow up on the chance he'd get a break, and let him stay in his room at the Greenbrier. The next day, the IRS man asked Sam if he paid for the room, and Sam said no, it was given to him for when he stayed there. The IRS man then told Sam that the room counted as salary and had to be reported on his tax return. Sam went through the roof.

Another time an IRS man showed up at Sam's door wearing a brown suit with white socks, and Sam didn't even bother with any efforts to ease the pain. He knew right then and there that anybody who dresses like that was not going to be the kind of guy who would listen to reason.

SPORTSMAN

Don Ryder, the head professional at the Homestead Hotel, knew Sam for over thirty years, and when asked if he could sum up his old friend in a sentence or two, he said, "I think of Sam as an outdoorsman. He chose golf as a career, because that's the way he could make his living. But he liked to be in nature. He loved animals and fish, all things in nature. The first time I ever played golf with him he asked me after the round if I'd like to come over to his place to see his trophies. I was thrilled to do that, and when we got there he showed me all the deer and bear skins and stuffed birds and fish that he had caught and killed. There were hardly any golf trophies showing anywhere."

When Atlanta sportswriter Furman Bisher visited Sam at his farm one day, he asked to see the British Open trophy—actually, the replica every winner gets to keep. "Sam said it was around somewhere, and he began looking for it and finally found it in a box stashed away with a lot of other stuff. He was more interested in showing me the deer heads, the skin of an enormous Kodiak bear he and his son, Jack, shot in Alaska, stuffed tarpon and other large fish of the sea that he had caught. The golf trophies were a kind of afterthought."

Sam's affinity with nature was seamless, an inherent element in his makeup. Bill Campbell remembered a story that reflects Sam's intrinsic understanding of animal life. It was at the Greenbrier sometime in the late 1930s. Liz Whitney, from one of America's wealthiest families, was fly fishing in Howard's Creek. She was wearing the finest outfit and using the best equipment, but was not doing very well. While casting her line she saw Sam come down to the edge of the creek with a small periscope you could buy in a five-and-dime store, and a small hand net. He put one end of the periscope in the water and dangled some grass in the mirror of its upper half, so that it was reflected in the below-water mirror. The grass apparently looked like a bug, and attracted fish that came to eat it. That's when Sam scooped them up with his net and threw them, with no hook marks, onto the bank. Whitney watched with amazement.

It was as though Sam knew what the fish and animals were thinking. He could communicate with them, somehow speak their language. Perhaps the most incredible tale in that vein is the one about Sam regularly rubbing the belly of a fish that swam in the pond just below his house on the hill. It was an old bass, and Sam would walk along the edge of the pond until he caught the fish's eye. Then he rustled the top of the water and the bass would swim over to him. Sam would get his hand under the fish's belly and rub it. "A lot of people didn't believe that he did that," said Carl Chestnut, a native of Hot Springs who worked for Sam on his farm for some twenty-two years. "Most times you hit the water and fish are going to get out of there. But that old bass with his big eyeballs would follow Sam around, and when Sam rustled the water it would come over and get its belly rubbed. It was unreal the way he had with animals."

Chestnut also recalled Sam's relationship with a goose that was on the farm. "Sam had an old goose he called Grandpaw. Usually a goose will grab or nip you when it comes close to people, but not this one. Sam'd sit on the deck of the house and holler 'Grandpaw,' and that goose would start squawking and wobble up and sit on Sam's lap. Sam would feed him corn, and talk to him just like he was human. Sam said he thought the goose knew what he was talking about.

"When we went hunting," Chestnut continued, "Sam had a way of walking in the woods so you never heard him. You'd never know where he was. He would sit out in the woods and listen for the wild turkeys, and when they gobbled he'd smile and knew just where they were. His dog, Meister, wouldn't make a move, and Sam'd say that turkey would come over soon. And it would."

Sam's most bizarre animal episode came after his celebrated exhibition tour of South Africa in 1947, where he discovered the putting wizard Bobby Locke (and was beaten by him almost every time). While there Sam got the idea to start a monkey farm in Hot Springs. To begin the project he bought two tiny South African Squirrel monkeys and brought them back to the United States. He secreted them under his shirt (and trenchcoat) in order to get them on board the plane in Johannesburg, and then through U.S. Customs. The monkeys scratched him bloody, but he got them through. He didn't go directly home, however, because it was the week of the Masters. He took a room in the Richmond Hotel, in Augusta, and left the monkeys in the room while he went out to play. The hotel manager was up in arms, because the monkeys were pulling the curtains down, swinging across the room, and of course shitting all over the place. Finally, Sam got the monkeys back to Hot Springs, and kept them in the basement of the house. They made a great mess there, too, and now had Audrey going up the wall. One day she was doing the laundry and "accidentally" left a window open. One of the monkeys got out, and was never heard from again. The other was somehow squished to death when something fell on it. End of the monkey farm idea.

"Tell you how much Sam loved to be in nature," said Don Ryder. "We were out fishing one day and it's raining hard, but he won't quit. He's fishing for all he's worth. I tell him, Sam don't you think we ought to go in? He finds a plastic trash bag, puts a hole in it, and pulls it over him like a poncho. And he goes on fishing. He wasn't catching anything, but he just loved being outdoors."

Sam ate a lot of what he shot and took from the water. He liked squirrel, which when fried tasted "just like pork loin," said Carl Chestnut. "Audrey would cook 'em up. She was good at it."

There is a fascinating coda to Sam's life as an outdoorsman, a hunter. When he reached his sixties he decided he would no longer kill a deer or other such animals. Wild turkeys and quail, yes, squirrels, yes, but no deer or bears. He came to the conclusion that these beasts were too beautiful to kill. It is something many hunters come to. But Joan Campbell suggested that it was Sam's response to reaching that time of life when he began to recognize his mortality. It might also be that he had simply matured as a human being, understood it wasn't really a fair fight between the animals and his powerful gun, and let them be.

DIRTY JOKES

In the days before radio and television, the people who lived in such isolated areas as the back mountains of Virginia entertained each other with homemade music and storytelling, a form of folklore that goes as far back as human history. Telling stories was how a people passed their annals down through the generations. Sam Snead was a master of storytelling, as were his brothers Jesse and Pete. Sam was especially good at it. In a way too good, because his repertoire, his inventory of material, was not exclusively but in very large part in the category of pure raunch. He told very dirty jokes— crude, vulgar, gross jokes. So what? It should be no more than a mere passing detail in the life of someone, hardly something to elaborate on. Lots of people tell dirty jokes, especially men; it's the currency of fraternity among some males. Except that in Sam's case it became something of a cause célèbre, because he very often told his dirty jokes in inappropriate company. This, in turn, affected his reputation in circles that confer honors on individuals.

For example, at Augusta National Golf Club there are bridges named after Gene Sarazen and Ben Hogan, but not one for Sam Snead, who won the tournament three times. Nor is there any other monument to him there that would present his name down through time. The general consensus is that people who run the Masters tournament omitted any memorial to Sam out of a fear that at the ceremony he would reel off something about a cow pissing on a flat rock, or tell about a famous bestiality trial held in south Georgia, and tell of the incidents in all their earthy details and *sans* euphemisms. Their fears were probably well founded. It was well known in the Establishment golf community that Bobby Jones was not very fond of Sam, and that this was mainly, if not only, because of his bawdy storytelling. Jones, who was himself a pretty good cusser, heard the stories every spring at the Masters Champions dinner. Gene Sarazen walked out of the room more than once when Sam got going, remarking that the "hillbilly was telling those dirty stories, and I had to leave." When Byron Nelson took over as emcee of the Champions dinner he allowed Sam to tell only one dirty joke per year.

But of course Sam spread his stuff around. One night at a dinner at Pinehurst, Sam was at the head table with Patty Berg and got to telling the dirty ones. Joe Phillips, the Wilson man, told Sam that Patty didn't appreciate it, but he went right on. Patty got up and left. On a couple of occasions in this writer's experience Sam was receiving an award at a dinner in a chandeliered dining room with everyone, including Sam, in formal dress—the women in fine long dresses and glittering with jewelry. When called up to accept his honor, Sam did a few nice thank-yous and then got down to business. Stories, with references to coprology, micturition, even a few not especially sly references to sexual intercourse. Often he used the most common terms for all the above, and always with a twinkle in his eye and an elfin smile as he reeled them off. He was enjoying himself. People squirmed in their seats, but alas, they also laughed and so he went on.

The same people in that fine setting who laughed at Sam's jokes would later denigrate him for his coarseness. "A bunch of hypocrites," said Mike Souchak, the burly tour pro who for years held the 72-hole scoring record on the PGA Tour, "because they prompted him to tell the jokes." Which was very often the case.

If Sam had limited his audience to the guys in the locker room or the men's grill, nobody would have said much about it. But the interesting question is what prompted him to tell these stories at banquets, and especially in front of women?

First, it should be noted that Sam was not entirely indiscriminate. He would never tell his jokes to Sylvia Snead, his sister-in-law. She knew of them, but insisted they not cross her ears. He did not tell them in the company of Bill Campbell, who is not entirely a straight-arrow prude but is someone who prefers a certain decorum in mixed social situations. "Sam always treated me like the fifteen-year-old boy he chaperoned to the North-South Amateur championship," said Campbell. "He was always very polite in my company, and that of my wife. Never off-color. But I did see the media fellows gather around him and prompt Sam to tell the jokes, and he accommodated them. They ate it up."

Ernie Vossler remembers a week he spent with Sam at the Mid Ocean Club, in Bermuda, filming a television golf competition. "My wife was along and we had dinner every night with Sam, and he never once told a dirty story," said Vossler.

Sylvia Snead was a much loved sister-in-law; Ernie Vossler was a good friend and fellow Wilson staff player; Bill Campbell was a longtime very good friend with considerable social graces. They were spared. Then why did he regale women he happened to be seated next to on an airplane, a first-date lady he took for lunch in Boston, and the nobs in tuxedos at banquets? How come he didn't pick up at some point in his long career of accepting awards on the refinements, the politesse, such gatherings demand?

Were his jokes in champagne company a kind of getting back at the social elite he caddied for and taught as a professional at the Homestead and the Greenbrier? He held a certain antipathy for the customers from up East, whom he surely must have perceived as looking down their collective nose at the hillbillies. He played out that aversion, at times. There is the story of a young Sam showing his annoyance at their big limousines speeding past all the locals in their tin lizzies on the way to and from the Homestead. The story goes that Sam refitted an old jalopy Ford to be the fastest automobile not on a race track, and when the big cars came down the road and passed Sam he revved up and zoomed by them going a hundred miles an hour. That'll show you, you stuck-up sonsabitches.

It could be Sam didn't even recognize the company for what it was, whether it was a gathering of the cream or the guys in the grill room. His niece Betty Dorn remembers that as a young girl she would be in the company of her father, Pete Snead, and her Uncle Sam while they sat around swapping stories. Pete had a taste for the off-color himself. Betty would tell them they ought to kind of clean them up, and "Uncle Sam looked at me in wonder, as though he didn't know what I was talking about." However, he and Pete did "tone 'em down a little" afterwards. Jack Burke Jr. had an interesting notion about Sam's stories, which he agrees were terrible. "He had a backwoods approach to life, and that came out in the jokes. The other thing is, the longer he was on the road the more unhappy he became, and telling the jokes was his way of getting back to where he came from. Besides, Sam being so famous, people would just roll their eyes and let him go ahead." In other words, he told them because he could.

There are jokes that express an attitude or point of view about the world, and are not just funny in their situations and in how they play out. Some of Sam's material might be categorized as making a social comment. It's a stretch to suggest this, but you might accept it if you're looking to give Sam a break and find some redeeming aspect for his vulgarity. For instance, Carl Chestnut remembers the first joke Sam told him. "It's about a guy with a real bad stutter. His friend tells him if he can order a pack of cigarettes down at the store without stuttering he'll give him fifty dollars. 'Fff . . . fif . . . fiffty dddd . . . dddolllars. Www . . . ow.' So he goes home and starts practicing, saying over and over, I'd like to have a pack of Chesterfield cigarettes, please, slapping his thigh all the while in a kind of nervous way. About a week goes by and he's ready. He goes to the store and says to the clerk, while slapping his thigh, 'I'd . . . like . . . to have . . . a . . . pack of . . . Chester . . . field cigarettes, please.' He did it slow, but got it right. Then the clerk asks him if he wants regular or filtered, and the fellow gets all red in the face and says, 'FFff . . . fu . . . fu . . . uck yyy . . . you!' Sam would tell that joke time and time again, and every time he'd laugh so hard tears came down out of his eyes."

One more, via Chestnut. "Guy goes into a whorehouse and says, 'I'm Big Moe and I wanna get fucked.' The bartender tells him to go upstairs to room number eight and slip a fifty-dollar bill under the door. He does that. The fifty-dollar bill disappears but the door doesn't open. Big Moe waits and waits. A half hour goes by. Finally, he beats on the door and says, 'My name is Big Moe and I come to get fucked.' The lady inside says, 'You mean *again*.'" Although those are only two of the thousands of jokes Sam told, one can see something of a pattern. Both the characters are being taken advantage of; one was thrown a curve, and in a sense cheated, the other was a simple-minded truster of people, albeit the wrong kind of people, and was taken for a ride. Not unlike a lot of things that happen in life, including Sam's. He had empathy for that sort of thing. He'd been raked over the coals more than a few times by wily businessmen, operators, writers of IOUs. Maybe there were some bitter drops in those tears of laughter when he told those jokes.

MONEY

The most enduring component in Sam Snead's reputation was that he was cheap, miserly, a tightwad, kept his money in tomato cans buried in his backyard. Claptrap. Bunkum. Sam had more than a little "poor mouth" in him. He liked people to think he was not well off, and in the early days of his career it worked. When he told everyone he went west to play the 1937 Tour for the first time and had only $300 in his pocket, it was believable not only because he was such a good storyteller but also because there was the Depression going on. Surely he had something left from the $10,000 he won in those two Tommy Tailer matches he had played on Long Island in 1935. He also had a contract with Dunlop, and some cash he had won in Florida and Nassau.

Like most country boys, or anyone from anywhere who knew some hard times growing up, Sam created the tightwad image as a defense mechanism against the many who put a touch on him once it was obvious he was in the money. It was a myth of rather sizable proportions. Sam Snead was an exceptionally generous man. If he knew you and liked you, and was convinced you really needed help, he was there for you. That he kept silent about his giving was part of the same defense mechanism; if it got around that he could be hit up for a loan, he would have hands reaching out to him from every direction.

However, it would not be right to say that protecting himself against would-be borrowers was the only reason he hid his charitable instincts. He was of a generation of athletes (or people in general) who did not trumpet their achievements. In Sam's era no one spiked the ball in the end zone after scoring a touchdown, then did a semi-obscene strut dance. When DiMaggio or Williams or Musial got the game-winning hit, when Johnny Unitas completed four passes in thirty seconds of playing time and pulled the Colts through to a victory, when Sam holed out to win the Masters, their reaction was controlled, understated satisfaction. A class act.

Sam didn't need to tell the world that one year he went to see the football team from his high school play a game, noticed how scruffy their uniforms were, and sent some money to the coach to dress the boys better. He also bought the entire team rings when it won the state championship. There is not a church in Bath County (where Hot Springs is located) that doesn't have a roof, an organ, a paved parking lot, or all three made possible by Sam's largesse. And yet, when a Virginia Supreme Court justice, Roscoe Stevenson, suggested calling the highway that runs through Hot Springs the Sam Snead Memorial Highway, the county board of supervisors wouldn't do it. They asked what had Sam Snead ever done for Bath County. While that issue was brewing, J.C. Snead ran into a girl he went to high school with, and the subject of the Sam Snead Highway came up. The girl agreed with the supervisor's position, until J.C. told her about all the things his uncle had done for the county. She had had no idea. Eventually, a state senator from Hot Springs went to the Virginia state house and got the proposal passed on the legal grounds that the sign designating the highway would be placed on state property. Done. (It's not the only thoroughfare named after Sam in those parts. Sam Snead Boulevard runs past the entrance to the Greenbrier, and Greensboro has a street named after him.)

Sam Snead was a Jekyll and Hyde when it came to his money. He had some odd quirks in the way he dealt with it. J.C. Snead recalled times when he would ask Sam for a sleeve of new balls. Sam scrunched up, hesitated, acted as if they were nuggets of gold. A sleeve of three golf balls! He got them for nothing all his life, by the thousands. Only after J.C. tore into him for being a Scrooge did Sam give him the balls—grudgingly.

On the other hand, one of Sam's favorite tour pro contemporaries was rotund Ed "Porky" Oliver, from Delaware. Oliver liked to play the horses, and when he wasn't picking them well he would run short of money. He would go to Sam, who would sign a check, leaving the amount blank, and tell Oliver, "Pork, try and keep it under five." Meaning five thousand dollars. Oliver always paid the money back. Sam helped many other pros in need. Up to a point. Al Besselink, a colorful and talented tour player who was also a notorious horseplayer, went to Sam periodically for some "fresh" to get back his own. He always paid Sam back, but after the fifth or sixth time Sam told Bessy it was getting to be a habit and he'd have to go elsewhere from now on. On the whole, as his friend Bob Girling put it, "Sam was a pretty soft touch out there."

When Oliver became very sick, had dropped to 90 pounds from the 230 he had carried and was clearly on his last legs, he still owed $6,000 on the house he would be leaving to his wife and their five children. Some Philadelphia club pros got together to raise some money for "Porky," and Joe Phillips asked Sam if he would come by to play an exhibition and give a clinic to help bring people and money in. Sam appeared, no charge. On the day of the event, though, it rained so heavily it had to be called off. But because the money had been collected, the pros felt obliged to make good on the exhibition, and rescheduled it. Sam said he'd come back, which he did. At his own expense.

Bob Goalby remembered Sam playing an exhibition sometime around 1978 at a club in Spartanburg, South

Carolina; the money raised was to go to the club's pro, who was ill and in need. Sam played and gave his fee, four thousand dollars, to the pro. He liked the fellow, who was hurting. Sam was very loyal to fellow golf professionals, the brotherhood.

Sam died a wealthy man, but he was not nearly as wealthy as he might have been. Out of a strange apathy or lack of interest that belied what people thought of his attitude about money, he didn't take full advantage of the many opportunities that came or might have come his way. He bought land, and owned a good bit over the years in the Virginias and Florida. He understood land. But as for stocks and bonds, or investments in oil leases and businesses, he did very little if anything. He didn't seem interested in amassing a great fortune. As long as he could go fishing and hunting whenever and wherever he pleased, had a quality fast car, could take care of his wife and mistresses in good style, and more than anything else could provide for his retarded son forever and for all time, he was satisfied.

For someone who would do a little semi-illegal wheeling and dealing for a $100 bet in a round of golf, he could be remarkably lax when it came to really big, significant deals. He was advised by Bob Girling to have Mark McCormack represent him. McCormack founded the hugely successful International Management Group, an agency representing athletes (mainly) that got its start handling the business affairs of Arnold Palmer. It subsequently grew into a multi-tentacled multimillion dollar enterprise. Even though McCormack would have come along rather late in Sam's playing career, he certainly would have made him far more money than he earned in endorsements and exhibitions or outings on his own. Sam decided not to go with McCormack. Why? Girling said Sam didn't like the idea of McCormack taking such a large cut of his purse money, something on the order of

25 percent. Girling told him that was peanuts next to what McCormack would make him in deals. "What's more," said Girling, "I told Sam that McCormack would do his taxes, bookkeeping, make his travel arrangements, everything. But Sam told me, 'Bob, I'm not going to do it.'"

"He needed someone to manage his affairs," said Girling, a great friend in Sam's later years. "I used to watch him do his books and handle his bills at home. There were stacks of papers all over his office, on the floor, everywhere. It piled up because he traveled so much. He'd sit there going through every bill, grousing about some guy charging him ten dollars too much. God bless him, but he never did grow out of the country boy he started out as. He had to do it himself."

As it was, Sam regularly sold himself short, charging five thousand dollars for an exhibition and dropping it to three thousand if he was paid in cash. He was bargain basement. This while Arnold Palmer, Jack Nicklaus, Lee Trevino, and even Chi-Chi Rodriguez were getting as much as twenty-five thousand dollars for a one-day outing. J. C. brought that up to his uncle more than once. "I'd say to him, 'Unckie,' that's how I usually addressed him, 'your name is as big as any of those other guys. You ought to demand the same amount, or somewhere near what they get. Why do you do that? It doesn't make any sense.' You know what he said? 'Well, it's just kind of laying there. I might as well pick it up.' I said, 'Don't you understand, if you sell yourself for five thousand and word gets out that they can get you for five, you aren't going to get any twenty-five or fifty. If you did one for fifty thousand, how many fives or tens do you have to do to make up for that?' He did nothing about it."

Sam didn't like to take advice on money matters. He'd go to all ends to find out what club a fellow who couldn't play a lick was hitting for an approach shot, but he wouldn't seek help from people who really knew their business and could help him when it meant thousands, maybe even millions of dollars. J.C. Snead, again: "Sam and Robert Trent Jones Sr., the golf course architect, owned a pretty good piece of property in Davie, Florida, right beside Hollywood. It must have been 250 acres, maybe more. They kept it for quite a few years, and every year when the tax bill came Sam would have a fit. He'd mutter something about having to pay $35,000 in taxes. I told him, 'Unckie, all you have to do is put a barbed wire fence around the land, put some cheap range cows out there, and report it as a farm. Your taxes will go down to practically nothing.' The land was already zoned for agriculture, anyway. He said, 'Who the hell ever heard of such a thing?' I said, 'I'm telling you Unc, that's how it works.' He says, 'Oh, bullshit.' And that was it. He wouldn't even check it out." Finally, Sam sold the property for about a million dollars, money he didn't need at the time and would have at least tripled if he had waited a few years. It was prime-location real estate on the east coast of south Florida. Maybe Sam didn't think his nephew was all that smart about real estate, and saw him as just a golf pro. But Sam had access to proven experts, and he wouldn't ask their advice, either.

"He had a couple of real good friends," said J.C. "Bob Girling, a real estate man who developed the huge King of Prussia Mall, outside Philadelphia, and Jerry Rich, of Rich Harvest Farms, in Chicago. One day we're playing at the Lower Cascades with Bob and Jerry. Sam and I get into a discussion about some legal thing having to do with real estate. I brought up an idea for how to deal with it, and he said, 'Oh bullshit, you can't do that.' I said, 'Unckie, go ask Bob and Jerry over there. They know a hell of a lot more about it than I do. They'd love to help you.' They would. They loved Sam. He said, 'Awww, I don't think so.' And he wouldn't do it."

"Another one," J.C. said. "He signed his last contract with the Greenbrier for practically nothing. A ripoff. He had a real good friend named John Vardaman, who usually went by the name Jack, a lawyer with a big firm in D.C., a good amateur golfer, and a guy who also loved Sam and would do anything for him. You'd think Sam would have had Jack look over the contract before he signed it. Nope."

Vardaman was more specific on the incident. "We were down at the Masters together and Sam was getting ready to sign on with the Greenbrier. His son Jack had gone over there to make the deal and wanted Sam to sign it. Sam grumbled that they weren't giving him enough money, and so on, so I asked to see the contract. He was hesitant. Well, he said, they only sent over the signature page. I told him to tell Jackie, or his wife, Ann, who was involved in a lot of Sam's business, to send the whole contract over for me to look at. He never did, and every time I saw him afterwards he bitched and moaned. I said, 'Well Sam, you didn't let me see it. Get it for me now, maybe I can do something.' I told him that slavery had been abolished and they couldn't make him work. He still didn't do it. Why was he like that? I just don't know."

Al Schwabbe had a thought on it. "I think Sam was too proud to ask people anything that would make it seem he wasn't smart and didn't know everything."

Although he was an average student in high school, Sam was not well educated. He rarely read anything other than the sports pages, did not have a great command of language, and in general didn't like things that were too complicated, or at all complicated. Put three thousand cash in his hand for an exhibition, and he was satisfied. He didn't have to pay taxes on the money, and he had it right there in front of him. Ben Hogan died a very wealthy man, not because his equipment company was a success, and certainly not from his purse money in tournament play, but from oil leases and other investments he was brought into by good friends. Jimmy Demaret benefited similarly from his friendship with businessmen. So did a lot of other golf professionals of that era. It was just about the only way to end up comfortable. Sam was never uncomfortable, not by any means, but because his career was so lengthy and his celebrity so great he could have been up there in pasha class.

But Sam was not compelled to live a life of yachts and private planes and great mansions embroidered with the artifacts of conspicuous consumption, to recall a term from his prime years. He wore fine shoes made in England for years on end, and repaired the frayed cuffs of his expensive sport jackets because they were still good. Sam wasn't cheap; he was thrifty, and there's a difference. The house he built on the farm in Hot Springs that was his home for the last forty years of his life is not significant architecturally—a nice white frame structure of generous size—nine thousand square feet—but not more than needed. The only extra, you might say, was an elevator Sam put in that rose from the garage to the third floor. He did it thinking ahead to the years when he might have back problems, and Audrey would be getting up in age. The most impressive thing about the house is the approach to it. It sits at the top of a long and gracefully sweeping swale that brings to mind Sam's golf swing.

From the very first days when he began to make good money, in 1937, he took care of members of his family who needed it. At the end of the 1937 season, after winning five tournaments and becoming the rising star in golf, he went back to Virginia and visited his sister Janet, who had married Cecil Stinespring and was living in Waynesboro, some seventy miles from Hot Springs. He found Janet living in a rundown house in a poor neighborhood, and took her for a ride into a better neighborhood with nicer homes. He saw a home that looked good to him, and to Janet, and Sam approached the owner, who happened to be painting the front yard fence. Sam asked him if the house was for sale. The man said yes, it might be. Sam asked how much. The man said $5,000. Sam went to his pocket and brought up the entire amount in cash. The owner of the house could hardly believe it. A deal was struck, and Janet raised her family of six children in the house. One of her sons, Pete, still lives in it.

Homer Snead married and had children he supported, more or less, with a radio repair shop he opened in Waynesboro. Homer was something of a free spirit. He might be working on a repair in his shop when some buddies would come by and ask if he wanted to play golf. Homer would drop everything, put out the Closed sign, and be off. Almost every time Sam came to visit Homer in Waynesboro, his brother hit him up for five thousand dollars. At one point, when Homer was in between things, Sam installed him as the golf shop pro at Long Boat Key resort on Florida's west coast near Tampa, where Sam had the contract. But Homer let all his buddies play for nothing, and take shirts and sweaters off the rack at no charge. Sam finally had to pull him out of the shop. But one way or another, Sam always took care of him. And of the medical bills for one of Homer's children, who had cancer.

When his brother Lyle became ill with emphysema, Sam took care of all the medical bills. Once Sam "got up," his father pretty much retired. Sam took care of his expenses and bought him a house in Hot Springs, where he lived after Laura Snead died in 1940. Family came first.

It was always written up in the press that Sam Snead had all his money hidden in tomato cans buried in his backyard. Nonsense, of course, but in a way he did something of the sort on a much bigger scale. When he bought the bank on the main street of Hot Springs to turn it into the first Sam Snead Tavern, he removed the bank's safe to his home on the hill and placed it in a basement-level walk-in room. He kept all his cash—the pigeon money and exhibition fees—in the safe. Only he knew the combination. When Carl Chestnut came to visit Sam one day after he had been dismissed from his job at the farm by Jack Snead, Chestnut told him he wanted to buy a house and needed seven thousand dollars for a down payment. It was money he didn't have. Rather than going through Jack and his wife, Ann, who were now handling most of his business affairs, Sam went down to his big tomato can in the basement, returned with the seven thousand in cash, and gave it to Chestnut.

Hardly the behavior of a cheapskate, a tightwad, a miser. More like a member of the fellowship of guys. That was all Sam Snead really wanted to be: one of the guys.

ONE OF THE GUYS

Jim Dodson, the golf author, remembered being in Greensboro, North Carolina, during the week of the annual tournament, and dropping by chance into the Lucky Two diner to get a bite to eat. Sitting in one of the booths was Sam Snead, with four guys he didn't seem to know, or had just met. He was telling stories, laughing, hanging out. No press people bugging him for a hillbilly one-liner, nobody hitting him for a loan, just hanging out with some guys.

Sam seemed to have had an ironic attitude toward celebrity. He thought it was kind of foolish to make a fuss over a fellow who happened to hit a golf ball better than most people, or ran a major corporation, or read the news on television. He thought golf was not that easy to do, and he expected praise for his ability at it, but outside of that he had his own value system. It was nonjudgmental. Ben Hogan, especially when he got into his seventies, was a conservative type who told the kids of the longhair generation to cut it off before they came around him. Sam couldn't care less if you had long hair, no hair, smoked pot, voted the Democratic or Republican ticket. If he didn't like the way you looked or talked or behaved he didn't criticize you, he just didn't have anything to do with you. Fair enough.

It follows that he didn't expect to be treated special. There's a lovely story in that regard from Don Ryder. He and his son, and Sam, were fishing from a canoe in a stream around Hot Springs. There were some shallow spots on which the canoe got stuck every now and then, and someone had to get out and pull it into deeper water. Ryder did this a few times, and his son helped him two or three times while Sam sat in the boat. Ryder's son finally got tired from the work, and when the canoe got stuck again Sam asked him why he wasn't out helping his dad pull it over the shallow. The boy said, "Mister Snead, I don't know if you noticed, but the canoe is dragging right where you're setting." Sam laughed and got out and helped with the canoe.

"A kid could tell him off," said Ryder, "and he'd take it. That's the kind of man he was." Another time, Ryder had a cookout for twenty members of a visiting golf club who were staying at the Homestead. He invited Sam and his friend Bob Girling, and they came. Sam told stories and sang songs, they ate, and then Sam said that if they were not doing anything they might like to come to his place and watch the fights. They wouldn't miss it for a minute, hanging out with the great Sam Snead. "How many famous guys like Sam would do a thing like that?" Ryder asks.

Dottie May Campbell, daughter of the Chicago golf tournament promoter George S. May, knew Sam when she was in her late teens. Sam and Johnny Bulla stayed at the May home when in town for the All-American and "World" Championship tournaments, in the mid-1940s. "Sam never did his dirty jokes with me," Dottie remembered. "I was like a granddaughter to him. He was a likeable pro. Some of the pros were a bit too full of themselves, but Sam never got the high hat, never played the celebrity snoot. I'll tell you one thing, he showed up one year in his sailor suit and he was one damn cute sailor."

There was a striking vignette involving Dottie May and Sam that shows how unsophisticated he could be. Dottie and Sam were sitting in the kitchen of the May home having a chat. There was a big bowl of fresh fruit on the table, and Sam mentioned how he enjoyed fruit but found it hard to get on the road. "So I said, Sam, there is a thing where you pick up the phone in your room and ask for room service. You ask for some fresh fruit, and they'll bring it right up to you. He said, 'You're kidding.' He didn't know about room service, and he'd been traveling for ten years by then." It makes you wonder whether maybe he actually didn't know how they got his picture in the *New York Times.*

Sam never expressed any political views and may never have voted for a presidential candidate; he had no interest in the arts; and he responded to particular movements in society such as the race issue only if he was somehow involved personally. Then, out of a sense of what was right, he could respond to an issue in a significant way. In this writer's book, *Gettin' to the Dance Floor,* Bill Spiller, an African-American golfer, told how he began the process of breaking down the color barrier that had kept men of his race off the PGA Tour. Spiller said some white professionals of the time, the late 1940s and early 1950s, were aggressively against blacks playing on their circuit. Others were helpful, including Sam Snead, which surprised Spiller, "He being a hillbilly and all," as Spiller put it. Sam did not play an active role in the movement that gave Spiller, then Charlie Sifford and Lee Elder, the opportunity to play major-league tournament golf. Sam once said of the issue, "It'll resolve itself." But Sam did step in once to help make a difference.

In 1963, when the issue of racism in the United States was at perhaps its highest heat, a bartender at a West Virginia golf club where Al Schwabbe was a member asked Schwabbe if the upcoming West Virginia Open was really open. Could he play in it if he entered? No black had ever played in the event. Schwabbe told the fellow to send in his entry and see what happened. He did, and the executive director of the tournament had no problem with it. Still, Schwabbe was a little concerned about what might happen when the fellow showed up to play, so he called Sam and told him the situation. "Sam asked me if the bartender could play, and I told him the fellow can shoot 75 on sand greens. That was good enough for Sam, who said they should pair him with him. Which they did. The guy was nervous as hell the first few holes, but Sam was nice to him, encouraged him, wouldn't putt out before the fellow did so the crowd wouldn't rush off to the next hole, and he eventually calmed down and played some nice golf."

The interesting thing about this episode is Sam asking, first of all, if the fellow "could play." He wasn't interested in a token appearance. In Sam's value system you first had to be qualified by ability, which seems to be a very sensible as well as honest way of going about things.

For Sam a good time was sitting around in the grill room or dining room at the Greenbrier with his friends— Lawson Hamilton, George Aide, the shoeshine boy from the locker room—singing songs. Barbershop quartet stuff, harmonizing on "I Want a Gal, Just Like the Gal Who Married Dear Old Dad."

One day, Bobby Fry finished a round of golf at the Greenbrier and drove his cart to the garage, where he saw Sam washing the carts down with a hose. Bobby asked him why he was doing that, meaning of course that Sam Snead shouldn't be doing such mundane work. Sam said he wanted to make sure a good job was done.

"He was happiest bringing in the hay, so to speak," said Joan Campbell. "If he was on a truck or climbing ladders or repairing something on the barn he would say that this is where he was happiest. He felt most himself in these circumstances. I think he was rather amused that he was famous."

6

MARRIAGE AND CHILDREN

IT WAS NOT A MARRIAGE MADE IN HEAVEN. IT WASN'T hell, either. It lived more or less in its anteroom, purgatory. It was a clash of fire and oil, of personalities that were, in some ways, too similar. Finally, it was a relationship ultimately shaped and deeply saddened by an unlucky childbirth.

According to Sylvia Snead, her brother-in-law Sam and Audrey Karnes were fighting and arguing with each other from the time they were teenagers. They fought or argued on the school bus, in the schoolyard, wherever, whenever. Not all the time, obviously, but a lot of the time. It seemed to run in the family; a kind of Hatfield-and-McCoy thing. Sylvia remembered that when Harry Snead heard the name of Elisha Karnes, Audrey's father, he repeated it with a kind of sneer. The favor was returned. No one knew what it was between them.

Audrey Karnes was the youngest of five siblings. She was born in Hot Springs and grew up on Hobby Horse farm, which was owned by Fay Ingalls, the president of the Homestead. The Karneses paid their rent by tending to the

Ingalls' farm and residence, which was immediately next door. Audrey prepared meals for the Ingalls' field hands, saw after their show horses, and also worked at the hotel as a maid. She grew to be a tall, solidly built, strawberry blonde as strong-willed as the fellow who courted her, on and off, from the time they were teenagers. Audrey sang alto in the school choir, was the valedictorian of her graduating class, liked to tell a joke, was an excellent cook, and was strong and athletic—at one point she carried a single-digit handicap and could hit well the toughest club in the bag, the 2-iron. So she and Sam had things in common—music, storytelling, laughter, golf, size. ("Sam liked big women, cowgirls, I called them," said his pal Doug Ford.) But they fought a lot. Or Audrey fought Sam. "Audrey was always married, Sam never was," as Sam's friend Al Schwabbe put it, referring to Sam's very active philandering that began when he hit the road to play the pro tour.

"Audrey was funny," said J.C. Snead. "She was lively, a lot of fun, but the moment she got with Sam, when those two were together, it was all over."

Audrey was smart enough that she might have helped Sam make business decisions and tend to family accounts, but she lived in a time when women were not allowed to get involved in their husbands' business affairs. That was the man's work. Audrey never even had her own checking account; Sam gave her cash to take care of expenses.

Audrey wasn't Sam's first choice. He had proposed marriage to a woman in Phoenix, whom he met when playing a tournament there in the late 1930s. It came close to happening, but the woman had second thoughts and opted to marry a local doctor instead. Afterwards, Sam went back to Hot Springs to ask for Audrey's hand, which is probably too formal a way to put it. In any case, he was hovering on thirty years old and anxious to get a family going. By now, except for Lyle,

Sam's brothers and his sister had all begun families. Each would have at least four children—Janet had six. Sam wanted to catch up, and have a big family like the one in which he was raised. But he never quite made it, to his lifelong regret.

Sam would have married Audrey sooner than he did, but his mother was very much against the match. She was so powerful a figure in Sam's life that he did as he was told, until Laura Snead died in 1940. That same year, Sam married Audrey. Sam was twenty-eight, Audrey twenty-six. The link was made in August, a week before the Canadian Open was to be played. They took their honeymoon in Niagara Falls, which just happened to be near the site of the tournament. Sam told Audrey, perhaps while getting rinsed by the water rushing off the cliff, something like, "Heck, Aud, they're playing just up the road. Might as well go see if I can win it and pay for the trip." It did. Sam won.

Sam took Audrey along on the tour for the first year or two after they were married, but it wasn't a happy situation. Sam told J.C. Snead, years later, that Audrey complained a lot about everything—the rooms, the food, the other pros' wives—and she wouldn't help Sam by making travel and accommodations arrangements. Sam finally got tired of all the grumbling and inertia, and quit taking her on the road. This effectively became a permanent state of affairs with the birth, on June 30, 1944, of their first child, Samuel Jackson Snead Jr., who for most of his life has gone by the name Jack, or Jackie.

Sam Jr. was born severely cross-eyed. Aside from the actual visual problems, the meanness of school kids toward physical abnormalities, a community resentment of all Sneads, caused young Jack difficulties throughout his school years. He was teased a lot. It wasn't until he was in his mid-twenties that his eye problem was eliminated. It didn't help that in his formative years his father was on the road as much as forty-five weeks a year. As a result, he was not very close to Sam even into his younger adulthood. Jack attended college, got married and had two children, and tried various business ventures. He worked in a pro shop for Sam, but only in the last years of his father's life did he have a close relationship with him. It wasn't Jack's fault, of course; it is what comes with the territory when your father makes his living on the road. Quondam tour manager Joe Black said Sam very often played every tournament on the schedule. And when he took a week off, he might travel to do some exhibitions or go on hunting and fishing trips.

Nowadays, tour pros earn so much money they can easily afford to take their families with them, at least during the months when the kids are on school vacation. Even then, they can fly home for a day or so between tournaments. To make it even easier, tournament sponsors provide the pros with courtesy cars, child care, and other conveniences. In Sam's day the grind was not only on the golf course. The pros of his era traveled by car, and even fast drivers like Sam couldn't cover the greater distances very quickly. And of course, because the purse money was slim, the pros had to stay out for weeks on end in order to make a decent living.

Audrey kept the house in Hot Springs and raised Jack while Sam was away. It was not the kind of marriage Audrey had in mind, but she had little choice. The domestic situation was manageable until the birth of their second child. Sam's mother had adamantly opposed his marrying Audrey because she detected mental problems in the Karnes family and was concerned they might show up in Sam's and Audrey's children. Betty Snead Dorn, one of Sam's nieces, remembered a time or two when "Grandma Snead went through the house fussing at Uncle Sam about it." Sylvia Snead also recalled that Sam's mother warned him that "you never know," referring to the health of the children that would come.

And so it came to be. Terence Dillon Snead was born May 27, 1952, and by most accounts of family and close friends who were there or thereabouts at the time, he was mentally retarded at birth. Johnny Bulla remembered that when Terry was six months old, "his eyes were dead; you could see right away that something was wrong." Al Schwabbe remembered Sam telling him the boy was born that way. "He had a big head, he just wasn't right," said Schwabbe.

Sam and Audrey would eventually say that Terence was born healthy, but contracted a virus and developed a serious fever when he was two years old that left him in his condition. Medical specialists say that's possible, but it is more likely this story was an effort by Sam and Audrey to dismiss any notion that a genetic defect was at fault. No one has offered a diagnosis, although Betty Dorn suggests Terence was (or is) autistic. There is some surface evidence of that.

According to Bulla, who was one of Sam's few confidants, a doctor told Sam and Audrey that Terence's condition came from Audrey's side, probably through her mother. Ida Mae Karnes did indeed have mental problems that were exacerbated later in her life. Upon hearing that, Bulla said, Audrey told Sam she would never let him touch her again, for fear, of course, that another child would be born with a similar defect. J.C. Snead corroborated that: "Sam told me that for the last forty years of their marriage they never had sex." That was a difficult decision for Audrey, given Sam's considerable sexual energy.

The burden of caring for Terence from day to day, as well as for Jackie, was left almost entirely to Audrey, although she did have hired domestic help. Sam was on the road most of the time. Terence, of course, was Audrey's biggest problem, and as he grew he became more difficult to handle. He was a big boy and very strong, and when frightened of something or just upset he could wreak some heavy damage. One time, frightened at the prospect of having a dentist treat him, he broke up a lot of equipment and furniture. As for the psychological side of dealing with Terry, neither Sam nor Audrey was prepared by education or training, and perhaps by their social milieu, to care for him; there was a certain shame attached to having an imperfect child in a world that lived so close to nature. Inevitably, it was decided to send Terry to the Devereux School, in Westchester, Pennsylvania, near Philadelphia, which specializes in caring for children with mental or psychological difficulties. Terry was at the school for some thirty-five years, although he spent the summer months at home in Hot Springs.

By all accounts of the Snead family (all the Karneses are dead as of this writing), Devereux was not a fortuitous arrangement for Terry. The consensus of opinion, albeit all of it from the Snead family and friends, is that the school did not give the boy the in-depth psychiatric care he needed, or even simply pay sufficient attention to him. The feeling is that he was capable of learning to do things, and could have become a more productive person able to live a somewhat fuller life. As Sylvia Snead put it, "That little fellow was not as bad off as they made him out to be. If you showed him how to do something, he never forgot it. He just had to be shown. He could do jigsaw puzzles, and when we went to the drugstore he knew where they were and went right to them."

"If they had done Terry right to start with, not Audrey and Sam, but the school he went to," said Buddy Cook, "they could have gotten him up to a sixth-grade education. And he could have stayed at Sam's farm all the time."

Carl Chestnut remembered that when he drove Terry back to Devereux after his summers in Hot Springs, all the valuable belongings in his cottage would be gone, stolen— his television set, radio, combs and brushes, sheets. "They didn't think anything of taking stuff from the rich man's boy," said Chestnut. "Every year Sam would have to buy him a new television and radio, and replace all the other stuff that had been taken."

Terry was (and is) something of an idiot savant in that he can complete jigsaw puzzles in hardly any time at all. Chestnut, who took care of Terry during the summer months and still visits him regularly, remarked on his knack for them: "He can do those puzzles, a thousand pieces, and real fast. He looks at it and says, it goes right there. He'll have two of them going at once. He always just needed someone to direct and teach him."

There were other such clues to a higher mental aptitude than was assigned to Terry, who was classified at Devereux as mentally retarded. Even Sam could be surprised, and saddened. As Bobby Fry recalled, "Sam used to bring Terry with him to the practice range. Terry didn't hit balls; he'd sit in the cart and watch Sam. One time the ball fell off the tee, and Terry said, 'Uhhh, uh, strike three.' Sam hit the next one, and Terry clapped his hands and said, 'Home run.' Sam looked at me and shook his head, as if to say, he's sharper than we think."

As noted earlier, Betty Snead Dorn thought Terry might have been autistic. Not a lot was known about autism in the 1950s, even in more erudite social settings; one can imagine that it was entirely unheard-of in the back mountains of Virginia. "I watched Terry closely," said Dorn, "and I thought the diagnosis about him that he was retarded was wrong. I had been around children with Down's syndrome and other kinds of problems, and have some understanding. You know, Terry wouldn't look me in the eye, and one day I said, 'Terry, I haven't seen your eyes in a long time. Do you think you could take that hat off'—he often wore a hat like Uncle Sam's—'so I could see your eyes?' He stood there for a long time, then took his hat off and looked at me kind of sideways. Then the hat went back on. [Reticence to make eye contact is a basic symptom of autism.] I told Uncle Sam once that if I could have gotten hold of that child a long time ago it would have been different. Uncle Sam kind of looked at me and didn't know what to say. Of course, by then it was too late. Terry was an adult by that time."

Keeping Terry at Devereux was expensive, and that brings up another instance of Sam's refusal to heed advice from others. Again, it was J.C. Snead who tried to help. "The cost of the Devereux school started out at a decent rate," said J.C., "but it kept going higher and higher until it got up around fifty thousand dollars a year, maybe more. Now Sam started complaining about the cost, and one day I told him, 'Unckie, there are people around the Hot Springs area that don't make very much money, and I know you can find a family, a lady, a husband and wife, that if you paid them twenty thousand a year to care for Terry they'd do flip-flops to make that much income. And they'd treat him right.

"Sam says, 'Oh hell, nobody is going to do that.' He wouldn't even check on it. And you know, in the end that's exactly what's happened."

In 1992, Terry was moved from Devereux to another school, in Roanoke, Virginia, and then, in 2002, to where he lives now, in the home of Steve and Pansy Gibson on a small farm about fifteen miles from Hot Springs. Pansy Gibson came to know Sam when she worked for him in the house on the hill after Audrey died. She cooked his meals and kept the house in order.

This writer had a personal visit with Terry and the Gibsons on their farm. They are a childless couple, and they welcomed Terry and have treated him like one of their own. When Terry came to the Gibsons he weighed close to three hundred pounds from eating poorly—candy bars,

McDonald's, junk food. In a few months the Gibsons got him down to a trim two hundred pounds. Facially, and in coloration, he seems to take after the Karneses. But there is some Snead in him. He's a big fellow, over six feet tall, with good posture, light on his feet, and of course very strong. "He'll stand with his hands crossed behind his back," says Pansy Gibson, "and lean around to see things, the way his dad did."

He speaks in a very low voice, usually repeats what is said to him, and then gives an answer, sometimes when prompted, other times on his own. He is a gentle man who does indeed avoid eye contact, but he will give you the occasional rather furtive glance. He has a toy plastic recorder with him most of the time, but no ordered music comes from it; he toots it. It seems to be more of a security object. And at times he sways from side to side in a rhythmic way to what you might assume, given the Snead family's connection with music, is an inner music. However, such swaying is another common symptom of autism.

Terry does his jigsaw puzzles and has an easy rapport with the pet dogs and cats around the farm. He seems content. How much more productive a life he might have had is not for anyone to say, certainly not someone without professional training. Any such scenario could be only a guess.

One thing is certain, though, Terry was a terribly heartbreaking part of Sam's and Audrey's lives. "It just tore Sam up. He couldn't handle the mental part," said Bob Goalby. "Sam would try to teach him how to drive a tractor, and the boy couldn't turn it the right way. He was very frustrated by it, and you could see Sam wanted to cry." He did, more often than people knew. Terry's condition had to be especially galling for a man whose personal culture was structured almost entirely on the physical, in which he took great pride, and who was himself so incredibly agile and strong.

Sports fans seldom if ever know what is really going on in an athlete's life that has an impact on his performance, and his comportment in public. Sam's manner in the years after Terry's birth was touched in ways by Terry's condition, of which the public knew nothing. "One reason Sam was always anxious about money is he wanted to be sure there was always enough to care for Terry, especially after he was gone," recalled Joan Campbell. Sam wasn't ashamed of Terry when the boy was home during the summer months. He often took him to local restaurants, to the golf course, and wherever else Sam had to go. But he never brought the subject up in company, and he made only the most passing reference to it in one of his books, which was co-written with sports psychologist Fran Pirozolla. One line, about a "younger son, who is still a joy in spite of his struggles."

With Audrey's decree that she would no longer sleep with Sam, he was given something of a free pass to continue, or expand, his sexual life with other women. As Skee Riegel noted, going back to his earliest days on the pro tour, "Everybody knew not to get a room next to Sam's, because they'd be up all night." To make a point of Sam's extramarital sex life here is not the result of Ken Starr–like prurience, or of an effort to capture the *National Enquirer* audience. It is done because this, like his penchant for telling dirty jokes, had a bearing on how Sam was regarded by the golf establishment. While on a primary level Sam simply didn't give a damn what the bluecoats at the USGA or the greenjackets at Augusta National thought about him and the way he lived his life—he was not about to kiss their rings—he was proud of his achievements and wanted the recognition those eminent bodies can bestow. But he was shortchanged to some extent because of his "indiscretions with the fair sex," as a veteran USGA man worded it.

Sam was not always very discreet in his affairs. He would sometimes show up at parties with a woman on each arm, and he might strut about with a coy little smile at the corner of his mouth that suggested he was proud of being the horny, rascally teenager who was making out. He could have used a little artifice in this area, but then he wouldn't have been Sam Snead. On the other hand, that there was little to no subterfuge in his playing around might be seen as a kind of honesty.

The wives of many celebrity husbands who are sports and show business stars, politicians, and noted business executives make a deal with themselves. They know their famous husbands are fooling around with other women, and they decide to let it be, make the best of it, and keep the marriage together for the sake of the children, financial concerns, or sometimes the husband's career when a messy divorce might damage his image. Or, because there is actually love between them, love that has a different tilt than the conventional kind but is love nevertheless. The latter seems to have been the case with Sam and Audrey. They loved each other, in their own way. Sam liked women, and he liked sex, and it was readily available. Audrey was well aware of this. She described Sam once to her son Jack as a "man's man."

For famous men like Sam Snead, women are always presenting themselves. Some women make a point of getting celebrity men into bed; a one-nighter is enough to fill out their card, so to speak. They are especially attracted to such men when they are built like Tarzan, as Al Schwabbe put it about Sam. It's hard for the men to turn it down, and not many do. Still, Sam never thought about leaving Audrey, and Audrey only thought of leaving once, as far as anyone knows. Bob Goalby remembers Audrey complaining about Sam's philandering and talking about divorce, until one of her woman friends told her she was nuts: "You've got two homes, a big car, a maid, all the money you need, and he's never home." Notion over. Good country sense prevailed. Besides, for people of their generation divorce was rare, not to mention harder to obtain.

What made the relationship between Sam and Audrey interesting, perhaps unique as this sort goes, at least in American society, was that there was no deception practiced. It was pure Sam Snead; it was all on the table. Not that he flaunted his lady friends in Audrey's face; he loved his wife and would never do such a thing to her. But she was well aware, and a certain kind of humor was played around it— Sam's kind, anyway. Carl Chestnut remembered a time when he was in the living room with Sam and Audrey, watching a movie on television that starred a well-known actress. "Sam was just watching Audrey," said Chestnut, "waiting for her to react. He knew what was coming. Finally she said to Sam, referring to the actress in the movie, 'I suppose you've been with her, too,' and Sam said, 'Naah, Aud, not that one.' Audrey goes up the wall, mad as hell. Sam laughs. But five minutes later Audrey's asking Sam what he needs, what she can get for him—something to eat, a drink or whatever."

Doug Ford recalled a story Sam told him about a time he and Audrey were watching a televised memorial to John F. Kennedy on the anniversary of his death. "They were saying something about all the girlfriends JFK had, and Audrey says to Sam, 'You'd make him look like a piker.' When Sam told me that I nearly fell out of my chair," said Ford.

Audrey never wanted for anything. Indeed, as Ford recalled, whatever Sam bought for his longtime mistress, Judy, he bought for Audrey, be it a new Cadillac, a fur coat, a fine watch, a house. His relationship with Judy seemed to be another odd-couple arrangement. Judy read widely, spoke three languages, and once had her own television program in West Virginia. But she enjoyed the company of this man who read almost nothing, seldom if ever went to a movie, had no political convictions anyone knew of, played golf all day, and would rather watch the fights on television than have dinner with the King of Morocco. And, in his later years, grumped and groused a lot around the house. "Well," Bob Girling suggested, "there are lots of other things besides intellectual interests that make a relationship work."

Judy was a tall, handsome blonde woman who had children from a former marriage. She sometimes traveled with Sam to tournaments and exhibitions, and she stayed nearby in Florida. After Audrey died, of cancer, on January 31, 1990, Judy lived with Sam during the winter in Florida and for a time in the house on the hill in Hot Springs. This last didn't sit well with Jack Snead and others, if for no other reason than it was thought she was only after Sam's money. She did have a notion Sam would marry her, but it didn't work out. Sam took Audrey's death very hard, harder than most people expected given the kind of relationship they had.

But even near the end they would go at each other. Audrey suffered a gradual decline in her health, and for the last year or so she never got out of her housecoat. She even wore it when she went into town to shop. She was advised by her doctor to get some exercise, but she had trouble walking; she wasn't able to lift her feet well, instead sliding them along the ground. Sam, sort of teasing, told her she had to lift her feet so she could get more out of the walk. Audrey came back, "Yeah, you old sonofabitch, you don't look so hot anymore, either."

"There must have been something there between them," said Doug Ford of the Sam-and-Audrey connection. He remembered that not long after Audrey died he went to Sam's house in Florida. Judy was there, and she told Doug that Sam was really in the dumps over Audrey's death. She asked Ford to try to get Sam out of the house for awhile. "I said, come on Sam, let's go play. He said he didn't have any shoes, and I said what, you've got a hundred pair stashed all over the place. He hemmed and hawed and I gave him a pair of mine, and we played. But he was not in it. It was the only time I ever saw Sam not into the game on a golf course."

Bob Girling saw his friend Sam cry twice, once when taking Terry back to Pennsylvania on a plane. "The boy was scared of flying, and he gripped Sam so hard, Sam remarked on how strong the boy was. He had tears in his eyes when he said it. The other time was when Audrey died. She was a good country woman who loved Sam, and you'd have to think Sam loved her, too."

7

THE SENIOR YEARS

THERE WAS A LAST HURRAH FOR SAM'S COMPETITIVE career, and it had an impact on professional golf not unlike that of his fabulous initial emergence on the scene in 1937. Once again, it was his magnificent swing that did the job. It regained the attention of the golfing public and propelled forward the case for a senior tournament circuit.

A bit of background history. Fred Raphael, the producer of the made-for-television series *Shell's Wonderful World of Golf*, developed an idea in the years after that program went off the air (in 1969) in which star golfers of the past would compete in a tournament he called *The Legends of Golf*. Raphael's timing was excellent. The country was in a nostalgic mood. Major League Baseball was having its Old-Timers Days, and Raphael thought, why not a golf Old-Timers Day? Three days, actually. *The Legends of Golf* was conceived as a 54-hole two-man-team best-ball tournament at stroke play. Jimmy Demaret was an important person in developing the competitive format, and also in convincing the players—including himself—to come out of retirement. The latter wasn't easy, at first. Proud athletes, they weren't sure they wanted to display reduced skills on national television. But the money was good, very good—a total purse of $400,000 for the first event, with the winners getting $50,000 each. Paul Runyan said to Demaret, after accepting an invitation to play: "Do you realize I can finish last and win more money than I ever won in any tournament I ever played in?" Runyan, by the way, was the first official leading money winner on the PGA Tour, taking in a grand total of $6,767 in 1934. And so, Demaret, Runyan, and the rest began to practice. Of course, Sam Snead was ready at a moment's notice. He had never stopped playing and practicing.

And it showed. In 1978, at the Onion Creek Country Club, in Austin, Texas, twelve teams teed off in the first *Legends of Golf* tournament. (Two years later Raphael found a sponsor, and it would become the *Liberty Mutual Legends of Golf.*) Sam and his partner, Gardner Dickinson, defeated Peter Thomson and Kel Nagle by one stroke, 193 to 194 on the par-70 course. The winning total was 13 under par, which itself was impressive even if two players produced the score (although Sam did make most of the birdies). But what made the showing really awesome to the viewing audience, and created further interest in senior golf, was Sam's swing and the quality of his game. At sixty-six, still trim (his chest never did sink to his middle), still able to pick his ball out of the cup without bending his knees, he took the club back high and far and struck the ball with a force and accuracy that belied his years. Who knows how many golfers in their fifties and sixties were encouraged after seeing Sam to keep playing and practicing, or at least not to give up the game. To top it all, although Dickinson did help on a couple of holes, Sam made six birdies in the last round to lead the way to victory.

Wow! These old geezers can still play!

The following year was the coup de theatre, although Sam didn't play a major role. In the third and final round,

Tommy Bolt and Roberto DeVicenzo got into a feisty duel, exchanging birdies on five consecutive holes and adding in some warm-spirited finger-pointing and needling. DeVicenzo and his partner, Julius Boros, won, but senior golf was the real winner. The television response to the tournament was so enthusiastic that Don January, Bob Goalby, Dickinson, Dan Sikes, and Boros set in motion the development of a tournament circuit for pros fifty years old and older.

Voila! The Senior PGA Tour began on a small scale with two tournaments in 1980. But what has been dubbed the greatest mulligan (second chance) in sports history has grown into a multimillion-dollar circuit. Sam, being Sam, did not contribute in the way of hard proposals, demands, contractual issues, etc. in the formation of the Professional Golfers Association of Seniors, the name of the organization before it became the Senior PGA Tour. But he played a very important role nonetheless. He was designated honorary chairman, and because he was the star of stars among the seniors it was important that Sam be on the scene whenever and wherever possible, doing public relations, as it were. He rarely missed meetings with television executives, potential and current tournament sponsors, and anyone else who might help the project. And once it got under way, Sam played in every event and attended all the cocktail parties that were important to keep sponsors happy. It was the kind of thing he wouldn't do when he was hiring himself out for exhibitions, but this was different. This was for the brotherhood of his fellow pros. All of which shows what Bob Goalby meant when, in his address at Sam's funeral, he emphasized how vital Sam was to the birth of the Senior PGA Tour.

The only thing Sam regretted about the advent of senior circuit golf was that he was not as competitive as he would have liked to be. He and his next partner in the *Liberty Mutual Legends of Golf* tournament, Don January, did finish second in the 1980 renewal, and in 1982 he and January won with a phenomenal 27-under-par total of 183. However, the *Legends* was not considered an "official" tournament when Sam won it, so in effect he never won a Senior PGA Tour event. So be it. His continuing presence was enough to help secure the viability of the circuit. Just watching him hit balls on the range was a good enough show, as it had been for all the years Sam was out there.

What's more, in its usual follow-up role relating to new movements and innovations in golf, the USGA was motivated by the interest developed in senior golf to begin the U.S. Senior Open, in 1980. Alas, the best Sam could do was a tie for sixteenth in the 1981 event, held at Oakland Hills, where forty-four years earlier he almost won the first U.S. Open in which he competed.

In 1995, when the *Legends of Golf* tournament became a 72-hole event, Sam and Bob Goalby teamed up and finished in a tie for second. A pretty good performance on Sam's part for a man of eighty-three. It was his last showing in a professional competition. He would live another seven years (actually, four days short of that), confining his golf to rounds with friends.

What does a man who had been so busy for so many years do with himself? From 1937 through the 1960s Sam Snead traveled millions of miles playing hundreds and hundreds of tournaments and exhibitions. When not doing his golf he hunted and fished from Alaska to South Africa and in many of the woods, oceans, and streams in between. And now he had, relatively speaking, not much to do. How did he spend his time? In the usual way.

One fall day in the late 1980s, when Sam was preparing to leave for Florida, Audrey asked him why he was going down there. "To play golf, Audrey." "Why bother?" she said. "You don't win anything anymore." "Because that's what I do," said Sam, with a chuckle.

Until the last few years of his life Sam played 18 holes almost every day of the week, and when he didn't play he would always hit practice balls. He hung out a lot at the Homestead's Cascades course, where he first played the game, and waited for his pigeons to fly in, literally. Lawson Hamilton would get George Aide and one or another old pal from the Greenbrier and helicopter over. Sam would be waiting for them at the landing pod. He had been warming up for an hour, and was ready to go. Still able to shoot the occasional under-par round, he usually clipped the pigeon's wings. After the golf they had long sessions of gin rummy. According to the Hamilton gang, devoted friends of Sam, he was an excellent gin rummy player. However, at the Pine Tree Golf Club in Florida, where the gin players are from the big cities of the Northeast and Chicago, Sam was given a rather different rating at golf's "official" card game. According to Bob Girling, the gin players at Pine Tree "licked their lips when Sam came around." By the way, Sam was a paying member of Pine Tree, and may be the only touring pro to ever actually pay out of his own pocket for a membership in a private club—and the only touring pro to win a club championship, which he did once, just to say he did. Then he let the members alone.

Back at the farm he stayed in tune with nature by replacing his big-game hunting habit with an interest in fruit trees—he grew some peaches and apples on the farm—feeding his old goose, rubbing the belly of his bass, shooting the occasional turkey, and doing chores around the farm. He'd drive into Hot Springs to check his mail, then hang around at the fire station telling stories with the local firefighters and anyone else who happened by. And with his beloved dog, Meister, he would hunt for golf balls in the streams and long rough of the Cascades course.

His son Jack developed the idea for the Sam Snead Tavern and opened the first one, in downtown Hot Springs, in 1980. It is just a few doors away from the drugstore where Sam had worked as a boy. Sam had nothing to do with the operation of the restaurant, but did appear there with some regularity to have meals—steak and potatoes, salad, a hamburger for Meister. People were thrilled to see the legendary Slammin' Sam when he was in the house, but his presence was felt even when his actual body wasn't. Jack decorated the walls with photographs of Sam, with clubs and balls he used to win this and that tournament or championship, and other artifacts. There are now fifteen Sam Snead Taverns, mainly in the Southeast and South, all decorated the same way.

Sam did some promotional work for Wilson Sporting Goods—print ads and a television commercial with Gene Sarazen—and he participated in *Golf Digest* instruction panels until the early 1980s. Sam was given the freedom of the courses at the Homestead and did an occasional outing, for which he was paid. However, he never had a contract with the hotel. Even though all the actors who perpetrated the hurt of the 1935 Cascades Open were long gone, Sam never forgot the incident and the treatment he received there when he was a young man starting out in life.

Things were going along well enough for Sam until the week of the 1992 Masters, when disaster struck. Sam was never the same afterwards. He always looked forward to his annual trip to the Masters, which was his last public stage. He, Gene Sarazen, and Byron Nelson were the honorary starters, hitting a driver off the first tee on the first day of play to open the proceedings. But on April 7, 1992, that trip up to Augusta, Georgia, turned into a nightmare. Sam made the drive from Fort Pierce by himself, and apparently unwittingly got onto a road, Georgia Highway 56, that he had never taken before. He thought he was on the road he always took. Just over a railroad crossing in Burke County there was an intersection with a stop sign Sam didn't expect. He had slowed down to go over the tracks, but then was beginning to speed up when he ran the stop sign and crashed hard into the driver's side of a car driven by Roy Jeffers. It was not pretty.

Jeffers, the father of five children and with a sixth on the way, was left a quadriplegic as a result of the collision. The incident fell very hard on Sam, although not nearly the way it did on Jeffers, of course. Sam deeply regretted having caused the accident and the injury to Jeffers. "Sam used rough language about everything, and would use racially tinged references from time to time, but he never did about the fellow he hit, an African American," said Jack Vardaman.

Sam greatly feared losing everything he had in the settlement. His liability insurance coverage was not as full as it might have or should have been, and he was led to believe he would lose his trophies, guns, the house, everything. This time, he let an expert take care of his problem. Vardaman, with the prestigious Washington, D.C., law firm of Williams and Connolly (and a ranking senior amateur golfer) handled the affair for Sam. A settlement was reached that took a fair chunk of money out of Sam's financial legacy—a seven-figure amount—but did not break him. Not even by half.

Sam was wearing nonprescription sunglasses when the accident occurred. His license did not require that he wear corrective lenses, but he was eighty years old, and his vision may well have begun to deteriorate. As well as his mental faculties. After all, he had been driving up to Augusta for many years, and this time he thought he was on the same road he always took. Who can say when the faculties of someone of eighty begin to diminish? Certainly not a body-proud person like Sam Snead. He shouldn't have been driving to Augusta by himself, but when asked why he didn't fly he said he'd have to rent a car up there anyway so he might as well drive his own. That's the rationale of a young man living from week to week. An eighty-year-old millionaire should be taking things a little easier. There was some foolish frugality in his decision to drive, and body pride, but it also reflected someone who had spent maybe a third of his life in a car and who actually enjoyed the long drives. They were a time to wind down, think things out, and especially be your own boss. Once, as a young man still courting Audrey Karnes, Sam finished the last round of the Texas Open, in San Antonio, started driving that night, and didn't stop until he got to Hot Springs. He went on a date with Audrey, then got back in his car and drove to New Orleans, arriving just in time to make his Thursday first-round tee time. He shot a 69, and finally got some sleep. He was in his twenties then, and perhaps in 1992 thought he still was.

In the collision in Georgia, Sam suffered a shoulder separation and a knee injury. He had some doctors look him over, but he did not have surgery to repair any of the problems, and for some reason did not pursue a serious rehabilitation. As a result, his golf began to go into its ultimate decline. All the more so when his vision began to deteriorate. It started with his left eye, but eventually both were affected by macular degeneration that in his last days left him almost totally blind. Ironically, his great friend Johnny Bulla had the same eye problem at the end of his life. Friends of Sam believe that the accident marked the beginning of his decline not only in his physical health, but also in his mental acuity.

In the meantime, the Greenbrier was anxious to get Sam back at the hotel. Sam vowed never to set foot on the grounds again until a certain executive who had treated him and one of his employees badly in his previous stint at the hotel was gone. When that happened, in 1993, he returned to the place that gave him his first significant job in golf. It was his third and of course last turn with the hotel.

Some of Sam's friends said of the deal with the Greenbrier that he was underpaid and overworked. He received a yearly salary and got a percentage of the proceeds from the Sam Snead Pro Shop that was established there, and from a Sam Snead Tavern that was also put in place. But, as usual, he made a bargain out of himself. Perhaps it was because he felt he needed to replenish some of the money the accident cost his estate. As noted earlier, although he complained regularly to Jack Vardaman that they were wearing him out and he was not getting paid enough, when Vardaman asked Sam if he wanted him to renegotiate the contract Sam declined the offer.

He was living on the farm and commuting to the Greenbrier daily to give a clinic, entertain at parties, and sign books from 11 to noon every day. Sometimes he was assigned to a par-3 hole where he would hit a tee shot for every foursome coming through to try and better. He might be out there for ten, fifteen, twenty-five groups. It was rather demeaning, really, for a man of his stature in the game; it's the sort of thing a middle-range tour player might do to pick up a thousand bucks on a Monday afternoon. Also, there were Sundays when Sam was called in early for an "emergency" appearance to entertain a business group. He had to cancel his own golf game with his buddies. What's more, the hotel sent him on promotional trips to Jackson Hole, and even Japan on at least two occasions to promote a property the hotel was operating there. Sam enjoyed the adulation he received from the Japanese, but they were long trips for a man in his eighties.

He was also bothered by a bad toe that he injured when, in a fit of temper, he kicked a door in the house at the farm. A nail was sticking out of the door, and Sam's middle toe on his right foot connected with it. It bothered him for some time, and when he traveled up to Allentown, Pennsylvania, one day to do an exhibition at the local municipal course at the behest of Bob Girling, the toe had become seriously painful. "It was really killing him," said Girling, "and Sam looked like he was staggering out there. But he put on a clinic, played 18 holes, then immediately after went to the hospital in Allentown and had the toe amputated. Fortunately, it was a middle toe so it didn't affect his balance. He could still walk properly and swing the club."

Doctors who did get to examine Sam at this point in his life said he had the innards of a forty-year-old, but in truth his fabulously resilient body had begun to break down. It was inevitable, of course, one way or another. The Greenbrier gig probably hastened things along. But he soldiered on. He was born into a generation and into a particular social setting that obeyed, if you will, the work ethic. You work for your living, and when you sign a contract you are obliged to make good on it.

It wasn't all downhill. Sam got some ego massaging. In 1994, Karen Bednarski, at the time the librarian at the United States Golf Association, arranged a special exhibit called *Sam Snead, King of Swing*. It was a display of many of Sam's golf artifacts and vintage photographs, and a remembrance of his career. The opening reception was on February 10, at Golf House, in New Jersey. Sam's Chicago friend, real estate developer Jerry Rich, flew Sam up from Florida in his private plane. Bednarski knew of Sam's reputation for the bawdy story and was prepared for it. But there was not a hint of it. Indeed, Sam provided a rather touching moment when he asked Bednarski a plaintive question, "Karen, how come you're doing this? I never won the Open."

For the 2000 British Open, Lee Trevino inspired a Past Champions Jamboree that included Sam, Roberto DeVicenzo, Peter Thomson, Ian Baker-Finch, and others with their names on the claret jug. On Wednesday, the day before play in the Open began, all the past champions played four holes of St. Andrews Old Course—the 1st, 2nd, 17th, and 18th. Sam played them all, of course, in a foursome with Justin Leonard,

Nick Faldo, and Baker-Finch. The highlight for him came when he played off the first tee and began his walk down the fairway to his ball. The huge, soaring spectator stand to the right was packed, and everyone stood and raised a wonderful roar of applause as Sam passed. Sam was moved, as well he should have been. And when he got to the bridge over Swilcan Burn at the 18th fairway, he received another ovation and, in return, danced a bit of a jig. His response on the bridge was typical of him. The event did not come too soon. By this time Sam's health had been deteriorating more rapidly. It began two years earlier, again on his annual trip to Augusta National.

On the Tuesday of Masters week, 1998, Sam began the annual trip up to Augusta, Georgia, from Fort Pierce. This time he didn't do the driving. His son Jack drove the Lexus LS 400. *Golf Digest* writer Guy Yocum was along to do an article on Sam. At the outset of the trip Sam was in the backseat telling stories about his days on the road playing the tour. He then fell asleep, but near Jacksonville he awoke feeling ill. He needed to vomit, and Jack pulled the car to the side of the road, where Sam let it go. He was shaky, but said he was okay and told Jack to continue the trip. His Florida valet, Joe Bachman, who was trailing in another car, had stopped to see what was going on. He felt Sam's pulse, felt for fever, and watched his man bend over gasping for breath. Sam thought it might have been something he ate. His speech was slurred. Bachman and Jack were worried, and wanted to take him to a hospital. Sam adamantly rejected that idea, and they got back on the road and made it to the Augusta National Golf Club.

Bachman and Jack took Sam to the first-aid station, where a cardiologist looked at Sam and sent him immediately to the hospital in Augusta, where he stayed overnight. The prognosis was that Sam probably had a TIA, a kind of small stroke caused by a restriction of the blood vessels leading to the brain, which deprives it of oxygen. It happens to people who are overworked. But stroke also ran in the Snead family. Sam slept well on Wednesday night, and made his tee time.

As Yocum reported in his article, the doctors at the hospital, upon examining Sam, were astonished to find no plaque in his veins, and that his blood pressure was that of a thirty-year-old man. Still, he was eighty-six when the first TIA struck, and there would be others as the months and few remaining years went by. It was especially painful for him not to be able to see. However, that didn't entirely bench him. He played some holes, and in one instance pulled off one of the little miracles that the great players seem so often able to do. Buddy Cook was along, at the Greenbrier; it was the last time he played with his old boss and friend. Sam didn't miss a fairway on the front nine, but was of course much shorter off the tee. "On this par-four ninth hole where he had always had an 8-iron second shot, this time he hit a 3-wood up about twenty yards short of the green," Cook recalled. "I was over the green. Sam couldn't see the pin, and asked me where it was. I told him it was about midway up on the right side. He asked how far. And I told him he had thirty yards. He took an 8-iron, and holed out. For a three! Man, he was something."

In the last winter of his life, Sam often visited with his old friend Lew Keller, who brought back to golf the Oakhurst Golf Course in White Sulphur Springs—perhaps one of the first golf courses in the United States, but overgrown for many years. Sam helped Keller get Oakhurst going again, and at one point thought of keeping all his career artifacts in the clubhouse. "I may have been the last person to play golf with Sam," said Keller. "When he got real sick, we would have lunch at the club, but too many people would come up to talk to him about his strokes and so forth. So we started going to a truck stop on the highway near Fort Pierce, where nobody knew him. He wore his hat, but the truckers didn't know Sam.

We'd sit in a corner and have lunch, and on the way home he'd always want to stop by the golf course and see me hit a few. Sick as he was."

Sam's last trip to Augusta was in 2002. He was very ill by now and probably should not have gone. Jack encouraged him to make his appearance, although he didn't need to be too persuasive. By this time Sam was mentally quite disoriented, as Jack Vardaman remembered. "Sam stayed with me at Augusta, and he was in terrible shape. Physically, he was okay, but he didn't know where he was. I set up an interview with George Solomon, of the *Washington Post*, but Sam couldn't remember anything; he couldn't remember having played the tour. It wasn't Alzheimer's, I don't think. He had had a series of those small strokes."

The last golf ball Sam Snead ever hit was on April 11, 2002. It was his drive off the first tee at Augusta National. Unfortunately, it was not vintage Sam; there was no more slam. He pushed the ball to the right, and it hit a spectator in the head and broke his glasses. On the surface it was an ignominious end to a career glorified by the wonderful way he struck the ball for so many, many years, but Jack Vardaman said, "Sam actually hit the ball pretty well, pretty hard. Just a little right."

Apologies were made to the gentleman who was hit by the ball, and Sam was taken rather quickly from the premises. No one but Jack and his wife, Ann, and a doctor ever saw him alive again. Jack and Ann drove Sam back to the farm, in Hot Springs, and told all those who wanted to come by to visit that Sam was not presentable and that they would be dismayed at his appearance. Two weeks later, on May 23, 2002, four days shy of his ninetieth birthday, Sam died, in his own bed with Jack and Ann at his side.

Sam died on a Thursday; the funeral was on Sunday, May 26. It was the week of the Memorial Tournament, in

Columbus, Ohio, and in honor of Sam play was halted on
Sunday afternoon between 2:00 and 2:10. A long moment of
silence. In Scotland, the British flag at St. Andrews was low-
ered to half mast in Sam's memory. At the funeral his friends
from the Greenbrier, Lawson Hamilton, George Aide, and
others, wore their Sam Snead straw hats. So did Bob Girling.
Among the tour players attending were Tom Watson, Doug
Sanders, Curtis Strange (whose father once worked as an assistant to Sam at the Greenbrier), and Mac O'Grady. Speeches
were given by PGA Tour Commissioner Tim Finchem, Bob
Goalby, Robert Harris of the Greenbrier, and his dear old
friend Bill Campbell. Campbell was especially eloquent, con-
cluding with the following:

> *He had a deep pride of place,*
> *He loved his family,*
> *He enjoyed his friends, and*
> *He exuded vitality until nearly 90—*
> *Altogether, a great life, for which we all rejoice.*
> *Now he belongs to the Ages, and his like will not be seen*
again!

FOR THE RECORD

INDEPENDENT RECORD KEEPERS, WHOEVER THEY MAY BE (no one has said), credit Sam Snead with a total of 135 victories as a professional golfer. For many years, he was credited by the PGA of America and the PGA Tour with eighty-four official victories. However, in 1989 that official number was reduced to eighty-one, as determined by a panel of selectors chosen by the PGA Tour who decided that three tournaments on the original list of eighty-four were no longer of sufficient consequence to be included. (I was a selector.)

It sounds confusing, to be sure, but for Sam the reduction in his total was another illustration of why he always felt he was never given proper recognition for his achievements. It only exacerbated his long history of distrust and sense of being ripped off. When the pronouncement came down that eighty-one was the new official number, Sam began to say to one and all that if they kept it up Nicklaus would have more career victories than he. Not likely, since Jack's official number is seventy. (None of these figures includes victories in senior tournaments; it's PGA Tour events only, except of course for the British Open.)

In any case, with Sam's gibe in mind, his good friend, attorney John Vardaman, wrote a lengthy letter in 1996 to Tim Finchem, the commissioner of the PGA Tour, arguing Sam's case for putting the number of official PGA Tour victories at eighty-nine. The letter, which will be part of this chapter, tries to define what is meant by official and clarify other issues in the matter. I will list the eighty-one victories as noted in the *History of the PGA Tour*, and to the right include tournaments not on this list that were included in the accounting of eighty-four shown in the 1986 PGA Tour Record Book. In the process I have found what appear to be some simple errors of omission. For example, the *History of the Tour* shows Sam winning two tournaments in 1957; the Record Book shows him winning none.

As for the total of 135 victories claimed by Sam and his most loyal supporters, there is no record I know of to account for all of the fifty-one additional victories on the PGA Tour (based on the eighty-four figure) that would get the total to 135, even though his British Open victory was not counted in the PGA Tour's list. It is assumed that there are a number of Virginia and West Virginia Opens, although he would have had to win those ten or more times. I leave that figure for others to check out. Counting his victories as a senior would maybe get him close. There were six PGA Seniors titles and five World Seniors victories. Let it be said, simply and unequivocally, that to date no male golfer has ever won as many tournaments as Sam Snead did, whatever the actual count, and it is not likely anyone will ever win more.

For the sake of perspective, the list of victories will also include the total purse money Sam earned for each of those years (except 1936). Also, a starred tournament (**) represents a Major title by current standards; (*) represents an "unofficial" Major, which is not only my judgment but also that of the players of the time, who were considering the quality of the field and the venue.

HISTORY OF THE PGA TOUR	1986 PGA TOUR RECORD BOOK
1936 West Virginia Closed (No official money)	
1937 Oakland Open Bing Crosby Pro-Am	Not counted, perhaps for good reason. It ended up an 18 hole event, due to heavy rains.
Miami Open Nassau Open St. Paul Open ($10,243)	
1938 Bing Crosby Pro-Am Greensboro Open Inverness Invitational (Four-Ball) Palm Beach (Goodall) Round Robin Chicago Open Canadian Open* Westchester 108-Hole Open White Sulphur Springs Open ($18,534)	Not counted
1939 Miami Open St. Petersburg Open Miami-Biltmore Four-Ball ($9,712)	Ontario Open
1940 Inverness Four-Ball Canadian Open* Anthracite Open ($9,206)	
1941 Bing Crosby Pro-Am Canadian Open* St. Petersburg Open	Not counted

HISTORY OF THE
PGA TOUR

	North & South Open*	
	Rochester Times-Union Open	
	Henry Hurst Invitational	
	($12,848)	
1942	St. Petersburg Open	Cordoba Open
	PGA Championship**	
1943	Tour suspended during WWII	
1944	Richmond Open	
	Portland Open	
	($5,755)	
1945	Los Angeles Open*	
	Gulfport Open*	
	Pensacola Open	
	Jacksonville Open	
	Dallas Open	
	Tulsa Open	
	($24,436)	
1946	Miami Open	
	Greensboro Open	
	Jacksonville Open	
	Virginia Open	
	Tam O'Shanter World Championship*	
	($18,341)	
1947	No victories	
	($9,703)	
1948	Texas Open	
	($8,980)	
1949	Greensboro Open	
	Masters**	
	Washington Star Open	
	Dapper Dan Open	
	Western Open*	
	PGA Championship**	
	($31,593)	

HISTORY OF THE PGA TOUR	1986 PGA TOUR RECORD BOOK
1950 Los Angeles Open*	
Bing Crosby Pro-Am	Not counted
Texas Open	
Greensboro Open	
Miami Open	
Inverness Four-Ball	
North & South Open*	
Western Open	
Miami Beach Open	
Colonial National Invitational	
Reading Open	
($35,768)	
1951 Miami Open	
PGA Championship**	
($15,072)	
1952 Masters**	
Inverness Round Robin	Greenbrier Invitational
All-American Open	
Eastern Open	Julius Boros Open
Palm Beach Round Robin	
($19,908)	
1953 Baton Rouge Open	Texas Open
($14,115)	Greenbrier Invitational
1954 Masters**	
Palm Beach Round Robin	
($7,889)	
1955 Miami Open	
Greensboro Open	
Palm Beach Round Robin	
Insurance City Open	
($23,464)	
1956 Greensboro Open	Dallas Open
($8,253)	

HISTORY OF THE PGA TOUR	1986 PGA TOUR RECORD BOOK
1957 Dallas Open Palm Beach Round Robin ($28,260)	
1958 Dallas Open ($15,905)	Greenbrier Invitational
1959 (No victories) ($8,221)	Sam Snead Invitational
1960 DeSoto Open Greensboro Open ($19,905)	
1961 Tournament of Champions ($23,906)	Sam Snead Festival
1964 (No victories) ($8,383)	Haig & Haig Scotch Mixed Foursome
1965 Greensboro Open ($36,889)	

Sam's play in the majors (the U.S. Open aside, of course) has an interesting pattern. As we've mentioned earlier, he was an excellent match-play competitor. It can be said that four of his seven majors were won at that format—the three PGA Championships, and the 1954 Masters in which he defeated Ben Hogan in a play-off. In his first Masters victory he showed an unusual (for him) ability to finish strongly. His last two rounds were 67s, and he won by three. On the other hand, two years later he was tied for the lead going into the last round and shot an 80 to finish tied for eighth; Hogan won it with a final-round 68 to win by two over co-54-hole leader Skee Riegel. What's more, in 1958 Sam led by three strokes after 54 holes and shot a 72 to Doug Ford's 66, and finished second by three. That was a pretty phenomenal round by Ford, though. The next year, Sam was tied for the lead after 54 holes with Arnold Palmer, and shot a 79 to finish thirteenth.

Sam's last-round average score in the Masters was 75.4.

As for Sam's regular tour events, he was much better in the semi-tropical South than anywhere else, winning eighteen times in Florida, once in Nassau. Overall, he won fifty-eight tournaments in the South. The significance of this is that the courses south of the Mason-Dixon Line in that era were in native Bermuda and St. Augustine grass. These grasses are of a thick, flat, and tough blade that lies flat to the ground. The blades interweave, and the ball would often nestle down in the gaps between them. You had to definitely hit down on the ball with your irons, be a digger, and have strong wrists to play golf on this grass. The greens were relatively slow compared to the bent grass north of the Mason-Dixon, and because of the way the blades lay there was a lot of grain to contend with in putting. A putt over dead flat terrain could break two feet to the left or right, depending on which direction the blade tips were growing; they always grew toward the sun, of course, and wise heads on tour were always aware of which way was west.

Also, Sam won about half his tournaments in the first half of the year. These included all those in the South and leading up to the Masters, which had Bermuda greens in Sam's day. Sam had a knack for playing on this grass, it would seem, although he didn't grow up on it. Bermuda grass doesn't do well in cold winter climates, so one might wonder if maybe the slower greens were more to his liking.

Finally, and I'm sure Sam would argue with this, six of his victories were with partners or teammates in best-ball events—specifically, the Inverness Four-Ball four times, the Miami-Biltmore Four-Ball once, and the Haig and Haig Mixed Foursome. Therefore, I give him only half victories for them. His partners certainly helped to pick up the slack on a few occasions when Sam faltered, and vice-versa. Indeed, Sam almost always partnered with Jim Ferrier, the Australian-born player who won a PGA Championship and a number of regular tour events, who, although not very long off the tee, was a superb putter.

One other thing. After Sam's fabulous 1950 season, when he won eleven tournaments, he was deeply disturbed that Ben Hogan and not he was chosen as golf's Player of the Year. Sam complained that Hogan won only once that year. When he complained about the selection he was told that he had won it the previous year, and the electors didn't want a repeat. What they were really doing was giving Hogan a sympathy vote, in light of his tremendous comeback from his near-fatal highway accident to win the 1950 U.S. Open. The reason did not mollify Sam, who was so depressed he cut back his schedule and even let it out that he might quit playing competitive golf. Of course, he never followed up on that notion. And while he was down about the matter, he did win twice in 1951, at the Miami Open and the PGA Championship.

The following is the letter John Vardaman wrote to PGA Tour commissioner Tim Finchem in connection with Sam's "official" record. It has been abridged.

Dear Commissioner Finchem:

I am writing on behalf of Sam Snead to request that you reexamine the PGA Tour's determination of the number of Sam's tournament victories. For the reasons stated below, we think the PGA Tour should credit Sam with 89 significant tournament victories.

The background for this request is as follows. Sam turned pro in 1934 and won his first tournament in 1936. Over the next 30 years he won approximately 135 tournaments, of which 84 were recognized as "tour victories." During those years, the Tour was run by the PGA of America, the predecessor to the current PGA Tour, which conducted the tournament circuit, established the rules and regulations, maintained the statistics related to the tournaments and, as part of that function, credited players with tournament wins. Each year in its media guide the PGA of America published a list of tour victories. Since his last victory on the regular PGA Tour, in 1965, and indeed up through 1985, Sam was always credited with 84 tour victories . . . which was generally reported in the golf literature.

In 1986, the PGA Tour, which in 1968 had taken over the responsibility for the tour from the PGA of America, had a history of the PGA Tour written. In connection with that history, it began a Historical Statistics Project which was the foundation for ranking players who had competed at different times throughout the history of the Tour.

As part of that project, the Tour made a determination of what tournaments would and would not be counted in the ranking. Rather than accepting the PGA of America's determinations of what it considered significant and thereby "official," the Project made its own determination of what was and was not "official." Some tournaments counted for the Vardon Trophy, certain others for the Tournament of Champions, and others for official money winnings. . . . In the final analysis, players were then given credit for tournament victories only if the authors of the Project considered the tournaments had historical significance.

That process resulted in Sam being credited with six victories that had never been included in his 84 total. Those six are: 1937-38-41-50 Bing Crosby Pro-Ams, and the 1952-57 Palm Beach Round Robins.

However, at the same time the Tour took away eight tournaments for which Sam had always been given recognition. Those tournaments are:

1939 Ontario Open; 1942 Cordoba Open; 1952 Greenbrier Invitational; 1952 Julius Boros Open; 1953

Greenbrier Invitational; 1958 Greenbrier Invitational; 1959 and 1961 Sam Snead Festival.

As a result, in its History of the PGA Tour, Sam is given credit for only 81 wins, three fewer than recognized by the PGA of America. It is now widely reported throughout golf literature that Sam won 81 tournaments. We believe that this is unfair to Sam.

First, since the PGA of America was the governing body of professional golf in the United States during the years Sam won all of his tournaments, it would seem that it was the appropriate body to determine whether a tournament win should count as a Tour victory. I know of no precedent where a new governing body, such as the PGA Tour, has re-characterized historical records so as to take away achievements recognized by the body which governed a sport at the time of the achievements. One can't imagine the Commissioner of major league baseball taking away several of Babe Ruth's home runs on the grounds that the stadiums were too small or the ball too lively.

Moreover, in appraising the tournaments taken away from Sam you can see how arbitrary these decisions were. Over the years he had always been given credit for the 1939 Ontario Open. Yet, that tournament is not listed in his current record because it was held outside the United States. The same was true with the Cordoba Open, which Sam won in 1942. However, in examining the victories given to other players one finds numerous examples of victories outside the United States. For example:

Gene Sarazen   1928 Nassau Bahamas Open
Willie McFarlane   1936 Nassau Open
Byron Nelson   1945 Montreal Open
Ben Hogan   1946 Winnipeg Open
E.J. Harrison   1958 Tijuana Open
Bob Goalby   1971 Bahamas National Open
Doug Sanders   1973 Bahamas Islands Open

We understand that the tournaments are no longer credited to Sam's "official" record, because the purse did not meet the minimum required by the bylaws of the PGA of America. For instance, the purse in the 1959 Sam Snead Festival was $10,000 when the minimum required was $20,000. However, the PGA of America always found exceptions by which it waived that requirement. Thus, we think it is clear, as apparently the PGA of America thought it was, that being these tournaments were at 72-hole stroke play and had an impressive field of competitors they could therefore be deemed "official." The participants in these tournaments included the best of the day. For example:

1952-3-8 Greenbrier Invitational: Ed Oliver, Julius Boros, Bobby Locke, Toney Penna, Ed Furgol, Bob Toski, Dow Finsterwald, Jackie Burke, Jr., Ben Hogan, Jimmy Demaret, George Fazio, Clayton Heafner, Doug Ford, Gary Player, Doug Sanders, Claude Harmon, Lew Worsham, Dave Marr.

The 1959-61 Sam Snead Festival: Mike Souchak, E.J. Harrison, Ed Oliver, Doug Sanders, Bruce Crampton, Al Besselink, Gary Player, Arnold Palmer, Kel Nagle. Among others.

The strength of these fields provides a sound basis for PGA of America to recognize them as "official" Tour victories. I understand the Tour is now reviewing the tournaments records for all years of the Tour, and I hope as part of that review Sam will be given credit for all his 89 significant Tour victories.

Very truly yours,

John W. Vardaman

The letter was written on January 25, 1996. To date, the PGA Tour has not changed its records to reflect Vardaman's and Sam's contentions.

ACKNOWLEDGMENTS

MANY PEOPLE GAVE ME GENEROUS PORTIONS OF THEIR time and memories and insights to this story of Sam Snead, and this is to express my deepest thanks for their help. Among the many, they especially include: Bill and Joan Campbell, Dorothy May Campbell, Carl Chestnut, Buddy Cook, Betty Snead Dorn, Billy Farrell, Doug Ford, Bobby Fry, Bob Girling, Bob Goalby, Frank Hannigan, Robert Harris, Lewis Keller, Byron Nelson, Joe Phillips, Skee Riegel, Bob Rosburg, Don Ryder, Jack and Ann Snead, Jesse Carlisle (J.C.) Snead, Sylvia Snead, Bob Sommers, Bob Toski, Jack Vardaman, and Ernie Vossler. And a special thanks to my good pal Nils Nelson, who gave the book a good prepublication read.

INDEX